In the early 1800's, despite centuries of experience, man had little control over his vessels on the high seas. Nature was still an invincible foe, captains were governed by outmoded traditions, and the sea itself was an uncharted waste of waters. Matthew Fontaine Maury, a midshipman in the budding United States Navy of 1825, was appalled by these conditions, and set out to correct them.

SEEKER OF SEAWAYS is the absorbing biography of this remarkable man whose genius in finding safer ocean passages saved mankind untold suffering and hardship on the high seas, but whose loyalty to his native Virginia during the Civil War brought him only exile, poverty, and obscurity.

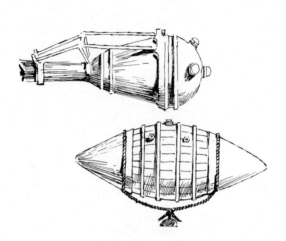

Seeker of Seaways

A Life of Matthew Fontaine Maury,
Pioneer Oceanographer

by Janice J. Beaty

ILLUSTRATIONS BY JOSEPH CELLINI

PANTHEON BOOKS

Library of Congress catalog card number: 66-12460

To
Billy

The sea, with its myths, has suggested attractive themes to all people in all ages. Like the heavens, it affords an almost endless variety of subjects for pleasing and profitable contemplation, and there has remained in the human mind a longing to learn more of its wonders and to understand its mysteries.

— Matthew Fontaine Maury,
The Physical Geography of the Sea

ACKNOWLEDGMENTS

I am greatly indebted to Frances Leigh Williams
for her extensive bibliography on Maury's life
and works; to the collection of Maury letters
published by his daughter Diana Maury Corbin
in *A Life of Matthew Fontaine Maury;* to
Maury Tuckerman, a direct descendant of
Maury, for his help in locating material;
to George Droste, head librarian at the Nieves
M. Flores Memorial Library, Agana, Guam;
and to my husband for his help and forbearance.

Contents

Seeker of Seaways

I ·

The Wilderness Road

THERE WAS nothing about Matthew Fontaine
Maury's early years to hint that his destiny
would be the sea. He was born a landsman on his
father's tobacco plantation near Fredericksburg,
Virginia. Long before he came to love the lazy Rappahannock River flowing down to Chesapeake Bay,
years before his heart would thrill to the sight of
slim-masted cargo schooners at Fredericksburg's
wharves, Maury turned his face away from the water
and headed inland.

He was only four and a half years old that crisp
fall morning in 1810 when his family started out for

Tennessee. Across the Blue Ridge Mountains and down the Valley Pike they rumbled, their farm wagons bulging with chests and barrels and children. There were Mary and Walker and Matilda and Betsy and Dick — all older than Matthew. Little Charles and baby Catherine rode with their mother and the womenservants in the front wagon where the dust was not so thick. The three menservants (as Virginians called their Negro slaves) handled the teams, while Matthew's father led the little procession from the back of a handsome bay hunter.

Nobody mentioned John, the only missing member of the family. They were still sick at heart that he had to go into the navy while yet so young. President Jefferson had granted the thirteen-year-old boy a midshipman's appointment only a year before. Now he was away at sea with little chance of securing a leave long enough to visit his family in far-off Tennessee. But hard times had come upon the Maurys. They knew they should feel relieved that the future of at least one son was secure.

Matthew's father, Richard Maury, would not admit to failure; he had come from too proud and distinguished a family. His distant Huguenot ancestors had held positions of influence in the French court. In England and colonial Virginia there had been clergymen and teachers and planters in the family. One wealthy and successful brother, James, was now the American consul at Liverpool, England. Two others, Fontaine and Abraham, were prosperous Fredericksburg gentlemen. And his late father, the Reverend James Maury, had been the inspired teacher of such notable Virginians as Thomas Jefferson and five signers of the Declaration of Independence.

Yet Richard Maury had failed. He could not make a living growing tobacco in Virginia. Worn-out soil, contrary weather, everything seemed to work against him, he complained. When at last his debts became too great, pride forced him to sell his land and most of his slaves in order to begin again, free from debt, in a new and more prosperous land. He turned to the bluegrass country of Tennessee, where Abram Maury, another Virginia relative, had already established a plantation.

It was a seven-hundred-mile trip through Virginia and over the Appalachian Mountains to Middle Tennessee. Yet their passage through the trim Virginia countryside might have been a holiday outing had they not been leaving their beloved state. Neat corn shocks and split-rail fences, hickory smoke and fresh apple cider filled them with images of Virginia they would never forget. They were graciously welcomed by relatives along the way, for the Maury clan was a large one. But at last they reached Salem, gateway to the mountain country, where the little party had to halt a few days to prepare for the difficult crossing ahead. Wagon wheels were checked and horses reshod. The family even spent a bit of its precious cash for the food and shelter of an inn.

They would be camping out from now on.

Then up into the mountains they trekked, along the old Wilderness Road through the Cumberland Gap. They were not alone. The trickle of pioneers moving west had already become a great flow. Some jolted along in billowing Conestoga wagons. Others trudged behind crude sledges on hickory runners. Mounted gentlemen passed cursing freighters, their whips cracking over straining teams. Peddlers and merchants led donkey trains through the deep ravines.

To young Matthew it was all a wonderful adventure. He was a fine-featured boy with curly brown hair and laughing blue eyes, but small for his age. They let him ride in a wagon on all except the steepest slopes. Then he had to hike along with the others to ease the strain on the horses. When his short legs grew tired, his sister Matilda carried him piggyback until she could tease him into walking again.

But even at this early age he was keenly alert and curious about everything around him: the sudden pop of a partridge flushed from underfoot . . . the sharp, sulfurous smell of homemade gunpowder . . . the rustling of dry oak leaves overhead . . . the cheery red berries of the mountain "burning bush" . . . the tumbling of white water down rocky-bottomed creeks . . . the howling of wolves at night and the answering snarls of their own hound dogs.

Twelve miles a day was all they could expect to accomplish in the mountains. They would make camp late every afternoon by a spring or near a creek. Then the children would be set to work gathering firewood or drawing water for the stock while the father and menservants went hunting and fishing. On Sundays they would lay over the whole day for the morning and evening prayer services of their Episcopal faith, led by their father. They were a deeply religious family that always began and ended each day with prayers.

The Nashville Basin region of Tennessee was just as lush and bountiful as Richard Maury had been led to expect. But there was no more free land for settlers, so the Maurys had to be content to work leased land for their first three years in the new country.

At last in 1813 they had saved enough to buy a two hundred-acre cotton farm six miles down the valley from Tree Lawn, their cousin Abram's plantation. The father then set his slaves and older sons to work cutting trees for their house. They laid it out on a rise overlooking the narrow valley. It was a solid and comfortable log dwelling with an open fireplace in the main room and a loft above where the children could sleep. Separate outbuildings housed kitchen, smokehouse, and slave quarters.

Seven-year-old Matthew delighted in life in the semiwilderness. There were woods to explore, animals to track, wild honey to find, and natural springs to discover. He and his older brother Dick soon knew every nook and cranny of their father's acres.

7

But it was young Matthew who led the way — who dreamed up each new adventure. One day they might ride over to the Harpeth River to see how far upstream they could swim their horses. Another time they might explore the Indian mounds and stone graves covering acres along the river bluffs.

Most often their father kept them busy in the cotton fields. Three slaves could not handle two hundred acres by themselves, and the father required all his sons to help. Matthew hated it. Planting and hoeing and picking field crops were no challenge to his adventurous spirit. He spent his time in the fields watching the clouds pass overhead, wondering where they had come from and where they were going; or listening for the ringing laugh of a woodpecker, and wondering if he dared search for its hole when he came to the end of a row. His hands and arms worked mechanically, but his heart was not in it.

Then nine-year-old Dick was sent to school, to an "old field" school (a one-room country school) near by taught by a single schoolmaster. Matthew was crushed. Not only was his beloved companion gone, but he was gone into the magic world of letters and numbers and books that Matthew longed so to know. As far back as he could remember, the boy had had a craving for knowledge. He was forever pestering his older brothers and sisters with questions they could not answer. What makes the thunder? Where does the river go? Why do the leaves turn red in the fall?

Asking his father these things only brought on the rebuke that children should not speak to their elders until spoken to. His mother had already given him home lessons: simple oral drill in Bible verses, Psalms, and hymns so that he could take part in their daily worship. But Matthew wanted more than this.

His persistence finally wore down his father, and he enrolled the boy in the school. It was the opening of a new world. To the end of his days Maury would remember the thrill of holding his first book: a Webster's Blue-backed Speller. The older children learned their history and geography aloud by rote, and the ever-alert Matthew soon mastered their lessons as well as his own. But farm work still came first with his father, and both Matthew and Dick had to let their lessons go when they were needed in the fields.

Then in the summer of 1814, John came home on his first leave. His five years on the high seas had been filled with extraordinary adventures, which he related with gusto to his wide-eyed brothers and sisters. The tall, sun-tanned eighteen-year-old had been serving as first officer on the *Pennsylvania Packet,* a China-bound merchant ship in the Pacific. Since the tiny American navy had so few openings for new officers, they were often granted leave to serve on such vessels.

Returning from China, the captain had dropped off John and four sailors with instructions to gather a cargo of sandalwood on Nuku Hiva Island in the

Marquesas. The *Pennsylvania Packet* would be back for them in two months. John described to his family how he had been befriended by the native chief Gattenewa, and told of the terrifying raids made by a rival cannibal tribe. Three sailors were killed before John could complete a sturdy tree hut high above the ground. There he and the remaining sailor had settled down to await the return of their vessel. It never appeared. Instead, a year and a half passed by before another ship entered the harbor. It was the American frigate *Essex* commanded by Commodore David Porter.

At first the crew would not accept the ragged, bearded John as an American naval officer. But finally a former shipmate recognized him. John then learned that America had been at war with England since June of 1812, that the *Pennsylvania Packet* was being held by the British in a Chinese harbor, and that Porter was returning to the States with several captured British vessels in tow.

John's story of his assistance in supplying the ships through Chief Gattenewa and of his new assignment as executive officer of the *Essex Junior* — as Commodore Porter renamed one of the British ships — held the younger Maurys spellbound. It ended with the great battle between Porter and a superior British force off Valparaiso, Chile, and told of the bitter defeat Porter suffered and of how the surviving American officers were allowed to return home.

Eight-year-old Matthew absorbed it all, storing the vivid tales in his mind to dream about long after John had returned to sea.

Still Matthew's aims did not turn seaward. Something else that his sharp eyes had spotted kindled his interest in a new field. It seemed that the cobbler in the nearby village was a mathematician of sorts. Lacking paper or even a slate, he scratched algebra problems all over the soles of the boots and shoes he was repairing. When little x's and y's began appearing on the Maurys' resoled shoes, Matthew had to find out what they were. He was delighted with his discovery of mathematics. Neil, the old shoemaker, was just as pleased to teach him as much as he could. Then and there the boy decided to become a mathematician.

But the old field school was no help. The schoolmaster had already taught Matthew all he knew. Brother Dick was now attending Harpeth Academy across the road from Tree Lawn, and Matthew begged to go too. His father refused. Money had always been scarce in the Maury household, and the expense of sending two sons to school at the same time was more than he could bear, especially when every available hand was needed on the struggling farm. The younger son's education must be sacrificed — just as his own had been. The father was the twelfth child in his own family and had never received a college education like his older brothers because there was no money left. So Matthew stayed in the fields.

Yet whenever his work was done, he and Dick continued exploring the wild countryside. Matthew developed a love for nature he never lost. Fishing and swimming from the Harpeth River banks thick with sweet gums, poplars, and willows . . . hunting squirrel and possum in virgin forests whose trees often rose forty feet to the first limb: these were the moments he lived for. Dogwood and redbud splashed the spring hillsides with color. Yellow jasmine and wild iris made the summer woods a garden.

Matthew was still the leader, always first with ideas for new adventures. One evening he decided to survey the woods from the top of the tallest tree. Dick watched with apprehension as Matthew disappeared among the branches over forty-five feet up. Suddenly there was a sharp crack, and a thrashing figure plunged to earth. As Matthew lay there, still and pale as death, the terrified Dick ran for help.

Matthew was carried home unconscious, with such a serious back injury that it would be months before he could stir from his bed. No more farm work for the lad, warned the doctor. It was the answer to Matthew's prayers, for now his father would have to allow him to attend Harpeth Academy.

As soon as he was able to ride the six miles to school, twelve-year-old Matthew enrolled. He was fortunate to come under the guidance of two outstanding educators. James Hervey Otey, another young Virginian, was not afraid to inspire his students with praise, unlike many teachers of the day. Matthew formed an admiration for Otey that would last a lifetime. William C. Hasbrouck, a young teacher from Newburgh, New York, also recognized the boy's ability and encouraged him in every way he could.

These were golden years for Matthew, and he prospered as never before. Legend has it that he mastered Latin in *seven days*. No doubt it was at this time that he developed his marvelous powers of concentration, which would later enable him to tackle and overcome the most difficult of subjects entirely on his own.

Then in 1823, John died of yellow fever and was buried at sea. The Maurys were deeply grieved, for only once in his fourteen years of naval service had he been able to visit them. John also left behind him a young wife from Fredericksburg and two children, none of whom his family had ever seen.

Matthew was by this time beginning to form his own future plans. In two more years his schooling at the Academy would be completed, but he was determined to further his studies, especially in science and math. Hasbrouck advised him to try for an appointment to the United States Military Academy at West Point near his own home town of Newburgh. It was one of the few American institutions then specializing in scientific subjects. Furthermore, the education there was free.

The idea appealed to Matthew, but he wondered how he could possibly convince his father of its worth. By now Matthew had recovered completely from his fall, and the elder Maury expected him to assume the duties of a planter as soon as his schooling was over. Any ideas to the contrary annoyed him no end. If Dick and Walker could accept their lot in life, why couldn't Matthew, he demanded to know? Nevertheless, Matthew again brought up the subject of further education. In a letter to a relative he noted the results: "I was anxious to enter the Military Academy at West Point. But the bare mention of the wish put my father in a rage. I abandoned the idea, therefore."

But he did not abandon the notion of somehow escaping from the cotton fields. His adventurous nature yearned for the world beyond his narrow Tennessee valley. His imaginative mind demanded a chance to seek and speculate and solve. So he turned to the one other obvious means: the navy. True, the navy had no formal school at that time, but its officers were taught practical subjects on shipboard. Then, there was the unfinished career of his brother John. Yes, its appeal was great. Perhaps, if he actually held a midshipman's appointment in his hand, his father would allow him to go.

Through friends Matthew secretly filed his application during his senior year at Harpeth. It was recommended by Sam Houston, his district's congressman, and granted on February 1, 1825. His parents were dismayed at the thought of another son lost to the navy, but it was clear that the young man was bound to go regardless.

His father was just as determined to stop him. Although he did not actually forbid his going, he refused to supply any money for the 750-mile trip to Washington, D.C. Matthew's quick wits overcame this difficulty; he persuaded a friend to sell him a horse on his promise to pay for it when he resold it at his destination. This solved his transportation problem. Then Hasbrouck saw to it he received thirty dollars pocket money for some tutoring he had done at the Academy.

On the April morning of Matthew's departure, his father turned his back on him and refused to say goodbye. But Matthew's worst moment came when he had to take leave of his brother Dick. The two had been inseparable, and he knew it might be years before he saw him again.

Finally Matthew mounted the gray mare Fanny and set out toward the old Wilderness Road he had traveled fourteen years earlier . . . toward his Washington, D.C. appointment . . . toward the sea.

2 ·
Aboard the *Brandywine*

MAURY'S ARRIVAL in Washington that June morning in 1825 went unnoticed. He was merely one of a dozen or so passengers disembarking from the little river steamboat up from Fredericksburg. It had been an overnight trip, but not even darkness could curb the excitement of the young naval-officer-to-be.

His month-long trip through Virginia had only whetted his appetite to know more of the watery world which would soon be his home. Every broad river of Tidewater Virginia was a highway to the sea. He had watched an endless procession of schooners and packets plying their trade up and down these waterways, carrying the wealth of Virginia's plantations to every port in the Western world. The warehouses at Fredericksburg bulged with furniture, silverware, yard goods, and wines brought back from Liverpool, Le Havre, and New York.

Every uncle and cousin Maury met along the way spoke of ships and the sea as if they were a common part of their lives. And so they were. For their world was built upon tobacco, flax, and grains which only deep water and fair winds could transport to distant markets. As for the navy, these Virginia relatives of his considered it an honor and a duty to serve as officers in their country's armed forces. Maury was delighted to learn that one of his Uncle Fontaine's sons was even now on the staff of the Navy Department in Washington.

Upon his arrival in the capital city, Maury went directly to the Navy Department, where he met this cousin, Richard B. Maury, and then insisted on reporting in person to the Secretary of the Navy, Samuel L. Southard. There, he was abashed to learn that his letter from the navy was only to notify him of his appointment, and not to order him to report for duty. However, Secretary Southard agreed to refund him fifteen cents a mile for his trip from Tennessee, which would tide him over until his orders were issued.

He stayed the summer with his cousin Richard, where at last he met his brother John's widow, Eliza, and her two sons. But his main thoughts and actions were occupied with his new career. Whenever possible he visited the Washington Navy Yard down on the Anacostia River about a mile from town. The great attraction there was a newly launched frigate, the *Brandywine,* being fitted out in preparation for its maiden voyage at the end of the summer. It had been chosen by President John Quincy Adams to transport the Marquis de Lafayette back to France at the conclusion of his present tour of the United States.

The beloved General Lafayette was being feted in towns and cities up and down the Union in grateful thanks for his services to America during the Revolutionary War. Maury had missed the Lafayette reception in Fredericksburg, but heard all about it from his Uncle Abraham, who had been on the welcoming committee.

Now he viewed the proud new ship with admiration. Its great black hull, glistening in the blazing sun of midsummer, was set off by trim bands of yellow around its gun ports, and matched by three towering black masts. Sailors scrambled aloft to hang its standing rigging and coat its stays and shrouds with tar. Officers in blue-and-gold uniforms shouted orders through little brass trumpets. Men rushed back and forth with buckets of tar, armloads of rigging, and bundles of canvas. Above the shouting and clumping came the piercing shrill of the boatswain's pipes. Maury yearned to be a part of it all, and soon.

He was not disappointed. On July 9 he received his orders to report for duty August 13 — on board the *Brandywine*! He was to be one of a select group of midshipmen whose relatives had served with Lafayette in the Revolutionary War. Pride in his rich heritage filled Maury's heart, for two of his uncles and one grandfather had fought in the Continental Army at Yorktown.

Before going aboard he had to purchase his uniform, a quadrant, and a copy of Nathaniel Bowditch's *The New American Practical Navigator*. Full dress for midshipmen consisted of a blue jacket with six brass buttons on each lapel, a standing collar with gold lace on either side, a cocked hat, white breeches, black leather half-boots, and a cut-and-thrust sword.

Maury was one of seven "acting" midshipmen who were rowed out to join the *Brandywine* on August 13 at her new anchorage in the Potomac. All together there were twenty-six "acting" and "warranted" midshipmen assigned to the ship for this special voyage. The latter were young men who had satisfactorily completed their trial period and had received their official "warrant," or appointment. A "passed" midshipman was assigned to show the new men to their quarters below. His title, they learned, meant that he had passed the examination required of every midshipman at the end of five years' service.

The moment Maury stepped from the gangway to the deck of the ship, his alert glance took in everything about him. They were on the upper or spar deck. As in all American men-of-war, this deck extended flat and unbroken for the full 175-foot length of the ship. Its sides, or bulwarks, rose to six feet all around to shield the deck crew from the winds while at sea and the enemy when at war. Twenty-four blunt-nosed carronades poked through gun ports in the bulwarks. Beside each one stood racks full of round shot and piles of unstowed gear. The area from the mainmast back to the stern of the ship was the "quarter-deck," they were told, and strictly reserved for the captain and higher officers.

Without further ado the passed midshipman led them down a hatch to the main or gun deck below. As soon as Maury's eyes became accustomed to the dim light, he saw that the gun deck was lined with the main battery of forty long-guns stationed at large square ports. To the stern were the captain's cabins and forward was the galley. They continued on down to the berth deck below. Here it was even darker, with the only light coming from two small glass ports in the hull and a skylight in the gun deck above. Even short-statured Maury had to stoop as he made his way along, for the heavy wooden beams overhead allowed less than five feet clearance.

Senior officers occupied tiny staterooms on either side of the aft section. Between these rooms was an open dining space for the officers called the wardroom. At last they arrived at a little compartment just forward of the wardroom, where midshipmen were quartered. This was the steerage, a section the width of the ship, but like a can of sardines for twenty-six active young men.

Each midshipman was assigned a two-foot-square wooden locker, a camp stool, and a hammock. Here they would sleep and eat, work and play for the duration of the voyage. But for the moment the steerage was a hubbub of men hauling supplies through a hatch to the breadroom, spirit room, ship's magazines, and the main hold below.

At last the great ship was ready to receive her honored guest. The morning of September 8 dawned gray and threatening, but the boatswain ordered all hands to fall in immediately. The marine guard and the band were called, and all officers instructed to assemble at once in dress uniform. Drums rolled, the shrill orders of the boatswain rang out, and men scrambled to their posts.

Maury and the midshipmen buckled on their swords, gave their boots one last polish, and hurried to assemble with the other officers on the quarter-deck above. As the commodore's launch bearing General Lafayette approached, the frigate's batteries thundered out a seventeen-gun salute. Despite the rain, which by now was beating down in sheets, the order rang out, "Lay aloft!" and five hundred sailors in blue jackets and white trousers sprang up the rigging and out upon the yardarms to give three cheers for Lafayette. It was a stirring sight, and a promising beginning for Matthew Maury's naval career.

His first day at sea was somewhat different. As the frigate left the shelter of Chesapeake Bay, immense waves began an endless pounding that soon had Maury and half the midshipmen seasick. It was no comfort to know that the great Lafayette was suffering too. At least he was dry. Water poured into the steerage from the flooded gun deck above, for the new ship's upper plankings had not yet swelled enough to become watertight.

But soon enough the young men were on their feet again and expected to carry out their duties. Passed and warranted midshipmen helped the others learn the proper routine. In their role of junior officers, they were expected to give orders to the sailors. But among the officers, theirs was the lowest order. Even the carpenter, sailmaker, and gunner outranked them. They were at the beck and call of every senior officer, and often found themselves treated as mere messenger boys.

Maury was glad to get out of the crowded steerage and assume his duties above. Every morning at four bells (6 A.M.) the roll of drums and discharge of muskets sounded reveille. The sailors had twelve minutes to "heave out and lash up," which meant getting out of their hammocks, rolling them up, and securing them with seven neat turns of the rope. Then Maury would direct a crew of sailors in washing down and "holystoning" the deck. Pulling the large, coarse-bottomed stone over the deck gave it a pale yellow appearance — the mark of a smart ship.

At six bells (7 A.M.) they were piped to breakfast: the sailors around squares of canvas on the gun deck, and the midshipmen below in the steerage. Ship's biscuits, boiled potatoes, and cold meat were their regular fare. But a sailor had accidently knocked an open bottle of turpentine over the midshipmen's sugar barrel, so their food tasted even more unappetizing than usual for most of the voyage.

At eight bells (8 A.M.) the band would assemble on the quarter-deck, the marine guard would march aft, and the colors would be run up to the roll of drums and the strains of a stirring march. Now the real work of the day would begin. Sailors climbed aloft to tar the rigging. Craftsmen began work in their shops between the long-gun carriages. The midshipmen began receiving instruction from the ship's schoolmaster in one of the forward cabins.

These duties could be interrupted at any time by the boatswain's whistle, piping all hands aloft to reef the topsails (take in slack) whenever the wind changed. A midshipman was in charge of each of the tops, and took great pride in leading the sailors aloft to give them their commands. All midshipmen, in fact, went by the name of "reefers."

Still Maury was greatly disappointed in the schooling he was receiving. The schoolmaster was a competent man who could have instructed him well in mathematics, English grammar, Spanish, and navigation, but he had no way of maintaining discipline. On deck the young midshipmen were model officers, for they were under the strict supervision of the mates and lieutenants. But in the classroom they suddenly became unruly schoolboys, full of pranks and ready to drop their slates and run at the first sound of the boatswain's pipes. The senior officers had little sympathy for the schoolmaster. In their eyes the "school of the sea" was the only one that counted.

Maury's second disappointment was in Bowditch's *The New American Practical Navigator*. Navigational problems were stated and their answers given. But Maury's ever-questing mind sought the reasons behind the solutions. There was nothing in the book to answer "Why?" It was more learning by rote.

Never one to be discouraged, he set out to learn navigation on his own. The steerage was no place to do it, he soon discovered. Skylarking was the rule there even more than in the classroom, and he enjoyed fun as much as the others. But during his two long deck watches of four hours each, he concentrated on learning something new every day. As he would write in later years in a letter to one of his relatives:

If I went below only for a moment or two, and could lay hands upon a dictionary or any book, I would note a sentence, or even a word, that I did not understand, and fix it in my memory to be reflected upon when I went on deck. I used to draw problems in spherical trigonometry with chalk on the shot, and put them in the racks where I could see them as I walked the deck.

Then on October 3, England was sighted, and on the following day, the coast of France. The midshipmen were sad to have their distinguished guest leave them at Le Havre, for he had spent many hours talking to each of them. As a token of their esteem they requested the American consul to send Lafayette an engraved silver urn in their names.

The *Brandywine* went on to England without delay. At Cowes on the Isle of Wight, she lay for two weeks while being thoroughly calked to end her persistent leaking. Maury and his mates were allowed to visit points of interest on the island. He was still enough of a landsman to be charmed by the narrow country lanes with their high hedgerows. But he was startled to see palm trees and subtropical vegetation growing at this latitude. There could be only one cause for it: this must be the work of the Gulf Stream, that strange warm current of water flowing all the way from the American tropics. He had read Dr. Benjamin Franklin's studies on it. He had even noted with interest its unique blue color the morning they crossed it. But now, seeing its profound effects at first hand, Maury was strangely excited.

Another welcome discovery in Cowes was a second-hand copy of J. W. Norie's *Epitome of Navigation,* which Maury found in a little bookshop and took back to the steerage to study. He had little time to peruse it. On October 22 they weighed anchor and set their sails for the Mediterranean. The *Brandywine* was bound to join the United States Mediterranean Squadron on patrol between Gibraltar and Egypt.

The great British fortress at Gibraltar was their first stop. For two weeks the *Brandywine* took her station in the harbor with several other ships of the American squadron. When the midshipmen were given liberty, they again took advantage of the sightseeing opportunities. Gibraltar's streets were alive with the colors and tongues of a dozen nations. White-turbaned Moors in flowing striped gowns strode past local water-sellers in breeches and doublets. Jewish merchants in black skullcaps and embroidered garments thronged to the daily auction in the square. Here and there a black-cloaked Spaniard sauntered past the stately British guards. Sailors from many lands roved the streets, spending all they owned in the grog shops.

Maury had no money to spend on the pleasures of the town — he was still in debt to friends for the very uniform he wore. But he did manage to scrape together enough to buy a Spanish textbook on navigation and a Spanish dictionary. Midshipmen were required to know Spanish as well as navigation. It was typical of Maury's efficient nature to learn both at the same time.

Then on the squadron moved, to its base at Port

Mahon on the Spanish island of Minorca. There Maury and his mates spent much of their liberty riding through the countryside on rented donkeys. Ancient trails led them through white-walled, red-tile-roofed villages, down to sweeping stretches of beach, and beside great stoneworks believed to be some four thousand years old.

Toward the end of February 1826, the *Brandywine* began her return voyage to the United States. Maury was ready. A longing to see his family and friends once more made him hope the trip would be a swift one. It was not. Contrary currents kept the vessel bottled up in the Mediterranean. Even under full sail she could make little headway. Seasoned hands told of being held up sometimes for months on end when opposing currents flowed through the Straits of Gibraltar. Again Maury marveled over the existence of such streams running through the sea. What caused them, he wondered, and what was their purpose? His books on navigation offered no explanation. Nor did the old sailors who knew the winds and waves of every sea. It was just the great empty ocean as it always had been, nothing more. But Maury persisted in wondering, and one day, in *The Physical Geography of the Sea,* he would write:

> . . . he who undertakes to study its phenomena must cease to regard it as a waste of waters. He must look upon it as a part of that exquisite machinery by which the harmonies of nature are preserved, and then he will begin to perceive the develop-

ments of order and the evidences of design; viewed in this light, it becomes a most beautiful and interesting subject for contemplation.

But for now, the most glorious sight in the world was the brooding Rock of Gibraltar at their stern, as they finally breasted the current and entered the Atlantic.

On April 18, 1826, the *Brandywine* dropped anchor in New York Harbor, thus completing her maiden voyage. An official warrant awaited those midshipmen whose trial period had been satisfactory. Maury was proud to be among their number. Yet when his first leave was granted, he was dismayed to learn he had only two weeks' time — far too little for the trip to Tennessee and back. Where would he go?

3.
Around the World

ALTHOUGH his family mattered a great deal, the State of Tennessee had no hold upon Maury. It was Virginia, land of his birth, that he longed to see most of all. This was the land his forefathers had settled. Their blood had stained its soil. Their labor had made it bloom. Its proud traditions and gracious hospitality were already close to his heart. From his mother he had first learned to admire its code of honor and gentle manners. At the homes of uncles and cousins along the way to Washington, he had come to appreciate its way of life. And Virginia in the spring . . . nothing would ever tug at his heart like white dogwood in greening woodlands, new colts in split-railed pastures, and dark green ivy on red brick walls.

Maury had until June 1 before he must report back on board the *Brandywine*. It was ample time to become reacquainted with his Virginia kinfolk, to ride and swim and fill up on the home cooking he had missed at sea. With genuine regret he left their stately homes behind when his two weeks were up, but ever afterward he would consider Virginia his only true home.

Back in New York he found the *Brandywine* in a flurry of preparation for a three-year cruise. So the rumors were true! His ship was bound for the Pacific to relieve the commander of the American Pacific Squadron there. Maury gloried in thoughts of the voyage they would be making around dangerous Cape Horn and up to that legendary sailor's paradise, Valparaiso, Chile.

On August 31, 1826, the *Brandywine* took advantage of favorable winds to begin her trip. She was accompanied by the new sloop-of-war *Vincennes,* a lighter but swifter vessel. The two proceeded rapidly to the outer harbor, where the wind suddenly died. There they lay for three endless days before winds rose strong enough to carry them over the bar and out to sea. Maury's impatience matched that of his 480 shipmates. They all knew that man's centuries of experience on the sea had gained him little control over his vessels. Ocean travel in the 1820s was still entirely dependent upon the whims of nature. Surely there must be a better way!

Once at sea Maury had little time to consider such problems. First he suffered his usual bout of seasickness. Then, as a warranted midshipman, he was required to guide the new acting midshipmen, as well as handle his own duties.

The first two weeks at sea were devoted to drilling crew members in their special-duty assignments. Station bills were posted throughout the ship, listing each man's station opposite his hammock number. Woe to the sailor found out of place! His name was put on the blacklist for punishment. Flogging was the most common form of punishment for sailors, but seldom for midshipmen. Being junior officers, about the worst they could expect was to be "mastheaded" — made to stand high on the foreroyal yardarm until called down. They could lash themselves to the mast to keep from falling, but in stormy weather it was a cruel ordeal. Stations were therefore learned quickly.

Next came the exercising of the guns. A lieutenant instructed each division in its duties. Then Maury and the other midshipmen in charge of the gun crews would call out names and expect every sailor to repeat his duties until all had learned them by heart.

Soon it was time for the midshipmen to begin their own learning. Their new schoolmaster was Inocencia de Soto, a Spaniard. The young men began their study of the Spanish language in high spirits, with thoughts of the pretty *señoritas* they would soon be able to talk to. All too soon their interest faded, as Señor de Soto did nothing but drill them over and over in the dullest of formal grammar. One by one the grammar books disappeared overboard until at last the distraught teacher gave up.

Maury was not sorry this time. His quick grasp of languages and previous study had already put him ahead of the others. To polish his pronunciation, he too preferred to wait and learn it first hand from the young ladies of Valparaiso.

Still, his disappointment in the quality of navy schooling was deep. After all, that had been his primary purpose in joining the navy. And by now his interest in navigation, especially its mathematical side, knew no bounds. But how to learn? the business of finding a location or plotting a course was often felt to be the private concern of the senior officers. In his column for the *Southern Literary Messenger,* Maury would later complain:

The Midshipman is practically taught to consider his attendance at school, as the matter of the least importance in his routine of duties. He is interrupted at his lessons to go on shore for the Captain's pig; or he is called from recitation, to count the duckfrocks and trowsers contained in the wardrobe of Tom Brown, the sailor. I have known a Captain, who forbade the Midshipman to "work out longitude," on the ground that it was a secret of the Captain and Master; and, therefore, it was exceedingly officious, and unbecoming the character of gentlemen, for Midshipmen to be prying into the rate and error of the chronometer, or to have anything to do with the longitude.

For the time being Maury had to be content with the practical knowledge he could pick up from old hands like the "sheet-anchor men." These were the oldest and most experienced seamen, assigned to tend all the sails on the bowsprit as well as the anchors and cables. From them he gained a great respect for the vast store of nautical knowledge they had gathered over the years.

They explained the *Brandywine*'s present zigzagging course to South America by telling of the treacherous currents north of Cape San Roque, Brazil. It was said that any vessel foolish enough to venture near their overpowering surge would be smashed to bits upon a desolate coast. A southbound ship must first proceed southeast across the Atlantic to the Cape Verde Islands near Africa. Then it could approach South America without harm by recrossing the Atlantic on a route that was tried and true. It seemed a waste of time to Maury, but the old sailors assured him it was better to follow a long, familiar course than a short one marked by dangers.

Now as they ran before the brisk northeast trade winds, the crew was turned out to scrub and polish and put the ship into the best order possible. Sailors were also required to keep close track of their own clothing and possessions. Anything left lying around the decks would be turned over to the master-at-arms, who kept it in the "lucky bag." Once a month the lucky bag was brought to the mainmast and the articles were returned to their unlucky owners, who always received several lashes for their carelessness. All this was in preparation for their first landing at Rio de Janeiro, Brazil. Man-of-war ships and crews were expected to look their smartest in a foreign port.

On October 25, fifty-five days out of New York they sighted land: little blue hills rising from the sea around an immense mist-shrouded peak. This was Cape Frio, the first landfall for all southbound ships approaching Rio.

Again contrary winds gripped the *Brandywine* and *Vincennes,* holding them off for two days before they could enter the harbor. At last on the 28th they stood in for shore, all hands in dress whites, ready to spring up the rigging and furl the sails at the order.

The *Brandywine* dipped her colors as she glided between the two harbor-entrance forts. Maury and his mates gasped in awe at the sudden splendor of the scene before them. No wonder Rio was acclaimed the world's most beautiful harbor! Majestic peaks bordered the landlocked bay, rising one behind the other till their lofty summits were lost in distant clouds. Neat white houses ringed the shore, nestled in groves of orange and lime. Strange little shallops and fishing smacks bobbed about the bay, all in the shadow of the towering black Sugar Loaf.

Their twenty-day layover in Rio was full of more pomp and ceremony than Maury cared for. He would rather have spent the time exploring the countryside. But all officers were required to stay on board to receive visiting dignitaries. Also, political trouble was brewing between Brazil and Argentina, and on November 18 the *Brandywine* received a note that the port was now closed to all ships either entering or leaving. Despite objections, the two American vessels sailed out of the harbor unhindered and headed for Cape Horn.

They would be crossing this difficult latitude during the Southern Hemisphere's summer. Still, chilling winds made the nights cold enough for pea jackets and mittens. Yet a summer "doubling of the Horn" gave them the advantage of long days. The sun would rise shortly after 2 A.M. and would not set until 10 P.M. the following night. To prepare for the ordeal ahead, the crew had to stow the exposed spar-deck guns and anchors below. Special storm sails were then "bent" (fastened) and all spars secured with extra-strong rigging. Maury later described the perils that awaited them most vividly in an article on the navigation of Cape Horn for the *American Journal of Science and Arts* in 1834:

There the tempest, the sea, and the iceberg assume

their most terrible character, each presenting dangers almost new in their kind and peculiar to the region. . . . The gales, frequently accompanied with hail and sleet, are proverbial among seamen for their unremitting severity, and the length of their duration. . . . The waves run to a height, which, in other seas, they seldom attain. In the calm they cause no less damage than in the gale, by distressing the ship with labor. In that succeeding a storm, vessels sometimes roll their masts away.

Despite the worsening weather, Maury manned the topsails and stood his watches like an old hand. But whenever he had a moment he began to jot down notes on the incredible changes in direction and force of the wind. Finding a way to overcome these obstacles was just the type of problem that appealed to him. The fact that no mariner in the past three hundred years had solved it did not bother Maury. The greater the challenge, the harder he would apply himself toward finding a solution.

The so-called inshore passage was favored by most captains, but the *Brandywine* soon found herself so buffeted by westerly gales that she could make no headway. Finally, by proceeding south toward the icy Antarctic, she escaped the worst blows and was able to make her westing around the Horn. Maury took special note of the *Brandywine*'s maneuverings, for his ship completed the difficult passage in only 17 days. Periods of 30 days were not uncommon, and

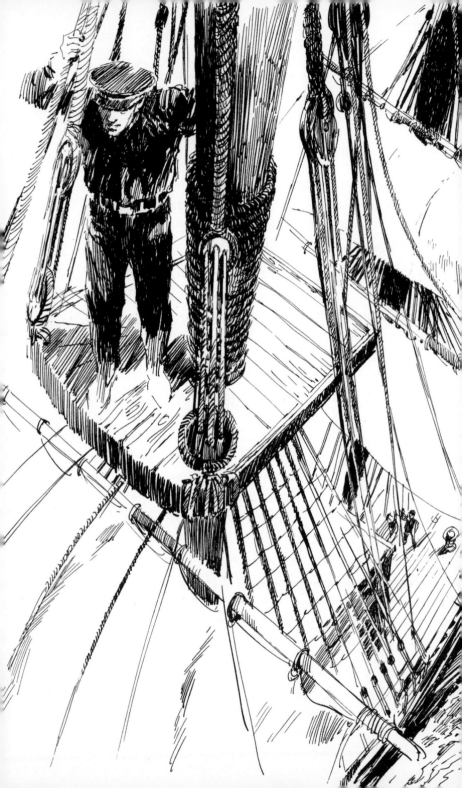

there were even records of ships struggling for 80 and 120 days to round the Horn, while some never made it at all.

On Christmas Day, 1826, all hands gratefully brought up the guns and anchors, repaired damaged rigging, and made the vessel shipshape for her entrance into Valparaiso. Everyone agreed that the Chilean port was truly a "Vale of Paradise" after the treacherous passage around the Horn. It was set like a string of jewels around a crescent bay, ringed by rugged hills and backed by the snow-capped Andes in the distance.

There was a brief liberty for the crew, but soon they were dispersed among the various vessels of the United States Squadron in the harbor and set to work again. Among other duties, Maury directed a crew in calking the brig *Columbia*. Then on January 24, 1827, the *Brandywine* proceeded on up to Callao, Peru, in company with the *United States*, the *Vincennes*, and the *Dolphin*. There Maury and his mates at last had their opportunity to learn Spanish from the lips of the *señoritas,* for several prominent Peruvian families invited the young officers into their homes.

Even more meaningful to Maury was his transfer in March to the swift little *Vincennes*. With fewer midshipmen in the steerage, he had more room to pursue his private studies. He was delighted to find books like Riddle's *Investigations of Rules and Principles of Lunar and other Observations.* Moreover, the captain, William B. Finch, was a well-liked officer in sympathy with up-and-coming young midshipmen. But the new schoolmaster was a decided failure. He ate too much, taught too little, and was finally put off the ship as a general nuisance. Again Maury was appalled. Was it possible the Navy Department did not know how poorly its future officers were being trained? He made a mental note to see that such facts were disclosed when he returned home.

The *Vincennes'* principal duty consisted of patrolling the west coast of South America from Valparaiso, Chile, up to Guayaquil, Ecuador, in order to protect American ships and property. Theirs was the delicate task of remaining friendly but firm in the face of restless political conditions and actual revolution. Maury witnessed real fighting during his two years' duty along the coast when the entire city of Guayaquil rose up in battle against a rebel political party.

Although he enjoyed watching this history-in-the-making, more exciting to Maury's scientific mind were his observations of nature at work. He would later note in *The Physical Geography of the Sea* that the strange Humboldt Current, for instance, caused remarkable things to happen:

In the harbor of Callao, in Peru, which is filled with the cool waters of Humboldt's current, I have seen the bay covered with a fog only a few inches high. I have seen fogs so dense, and with outlines so sharp, as to conceal from view the rowboats approaching the ship's side. These fogs, especially early in the morning, are sometimes so thick as to conceal from view not only the boat, but the persons of the crew up to the neck, so as to leave nothing visible but two rows of trunkless heads . . . skimming through the air and dancing on the fog in a manner at once both magical and fantastic.

As the *Vincennes'* tour of duty drew to a close in 1829, a new rumor began circulating: instead of returning home around Cape Horn, the ship was to cross the Pacific and continue home around Africa's Cape of Good Hope. She would then be the first American naval vessel to have circumnavigated the globe.

Maury's joy was complete when he learned they were heading first for the Marquesas Islands where his brother had been marooned for a year. It was also his good fortune to catch the attention of the ship's chaplain, the Reverend Charles Stewart. Stewart had been a missionary in the Sandwich Islands (Hawaii) and was well acquainted with the Polynesian languages and customs. He had quickly taken note of Maury's serious nature and intense interest in his surroundings. By the time they sighted Nuku Hiva in the Marquesas, the two of them were on excellent terms. Thereafter Stewart arranged for Maury to accompany expeditions on shore whenever possible.

They anchored in a deeply curved tropical bay opposite the village of Taiohae, home of the Happa tribe. The quiet beauty of the island was as overwhelming to Maury as the grandeur of Rio or the Andes or the vast Pacific itself. Slender coconut palms and sturdy breadfruit trees dotted the village like trees in a park. Maury marveled at the skill of its primitive builders, who raised their homes of bamboo and thatch upon massive stone platforms ten feet high.

On one expedition Stewart took along the entire ship's band to entertain them while they picnicked in a tropical glen. It was soon filled with hordes of curious Happas, attracted by the music. On another trip into a step-walled northern valley, they sighted fierce Typee warriors brandishing ironwood war clubs from the top of a cliff above them. It was merely a warning to their Happa guides to stay out of Typee territory.

All this time Maury had been memorizing Happa words in an effort to learn more about his brother's visit seventeen years earlier. Finally on the last week of their stay, an old chief was brought aboard the *Vincennes* to serve as a friendly hostage until all the sailors on shore had returned safely to the ship. Maury was then assigned to take the chief back to his village. To his great joy he discovered the old man to be Gattenawa, his brother's benefactor. Gattenawa was so pleased to meet the younger Maury that he offered him his scepter, his wife, and the daughter of a neighboring chief, if only he would stay! But the *Vincennes* and Maury departed on schedule after a spectacular night-long display of fireworks put on for the natives. They were bound for Otaheite (Tahiti) in the Society Islands.

Maury was charmed by the South Seas, but more than that, he was experiencing first hand all the problems and tricks of navigation in still another part of the world. He found that the very clouds overhead played an important role:

> Not only are these cloud-piles found capping the hills among the islands, but they are often seen to overhang the lowest islet of the tropics, and even to stand above coral patches and hidden reefs, "a cloud by day," to serve as a beacon to the lonely mariner out there at sea, and to warn him of the shoals and dangers which no lead or seaman's eye has ever seen or sounded out.

After a month's stay in Otaheite the *Vincennes* set sail for still another tropical island group, the Sandwich Islands, called by the natives "Owhyhee" (Hawaii). The Bay of Waikiki was not so strikingly beautiful as their previous tropical anchorages, but it was large and safe. Honolulu, they found, was already on its way to becoming a white man's town. Along with the fort and the king's palace were many missionary houses, chapels, and schools. Even the natives showed the Western influence. Women walked about in long loose gowns, covering them from neck to ankle, while the men wore poncholike garments hanging down to their loincloths.

Their stay in the Sandwich Islands was a pleasant one, with horseback trips into the countryside and social affairs to which the native royalty were invited. Maury was especially impressed with the graceful young Princess Nakienaena. Taking leave would have been difficult without the Orient and Africa still ahead.

The *Vincennes* finally weighed anchor for China on November 23. On December 19 they sighted the Spanish-owned Ladrones (Mariana Islands) but passed on without stopping. At last on the first day of the new year, 1830, they anchored off Macao on the South China Sea.

Captain Finch was invited by one of the American trading companies there to visit its "factory" (business house) in Canton, seventy miles up the Pearl River. He chose thirteen officers to accompany him. One was Midshipman Maury, by now a favorite of the captain because of his devotion to duty and great interest in every new sight to be seen. There were many on this upriver trip. Sampans, junks, and Tartar duck-boats crowded the river itself. Pagodas, forts, walled villages, and rice paddies lined its banks. Memories of this trip would one day make Maury's geography books come alive for generations of children.

They continued on to Manila in the Philippines and then through the Strait of Malacca and across the Indian Ocean to Capetown, South Africa, fifty-six days away. It might have been a tedious trip had not Maury kept himself occupied every spare moment by studying the new books he had acquired.

Euclid's rudiments of geometry and Laplace's higher mathematics gave him a broader foundation for solving the navigational problems that now absorbed him so. To guide a ship across the trackless sea, he had to be able to determine its position accurately at any time of day or night. Finding longitude, its east-west position, was the most difficult. It meant mastering nautical astronomy so that sights could be taken of various stars and planets. It meant learning to compute the acquired measurements. But Maury's pleasure in problem solving led him to delve far deeper than necessary. He spent his odd moments on the Indian Ocean, for instance, in devising an apparatus for taking accurate sights of the moon and then working out his own set of lunar tables.

That mere numbers scratched across a paper could actually plot the position of a tiny vessel in a vast ocean never failed to thrill Maury. Here at last was the practical application, the fulfillment, of his early love for mathematics. He began concentrating on each of the several methods for finding latitude and longitude, to discover its strengths and weaknesses. It was difficult work on his own, but how much better prepared he would be for his approaching fifth-year midshipman's examination . . . or so he thought.

By April 19 they were on their last leg home. Maury found himself gripped again by the familiar longing to see his family and state after four years at sea. Only one brief stop stood between them and their home port of New York. It was a disquieting one. The British island of St. Helena, two hundred miles off the west coast of Africa, was a pleasant enough place. Longwood House, where Napoleon had died nine years earlier, was interesting enough to visit. But it was here that Maury felt the first doubts that would one day overcome him and his entire country: what to do about slavery.

Great Britain was attempting to halt the slave trade by patrolling the west coast of Africa. Any slave vessels caught were destroyed, the Africans returned to their land, and the slaver crews dumped on St. Helena. Here they spent their days plotting to get back into their extremely profitable business again. Whenever more than a hundred of them had accumulated, they were shipped over to South America where they could cause less trouble. Maury shook his head at the sight of them, but had no better solution to offer.

On June 8, 1830, the *Vincennes* at last stood in to upper New York harbor, the first American naval vessel to sail around the world. Four days later a triumphant Matthew Maury planted his legs firmly on American soil with a broad grin across his face and a three month's leave ahead of him. His prospects could not have been brighter: three months to relax with his family; then the midshipman's examination which he was sure to pass with honors. How could he possibly miss the brilliant and carefree naval career that seemed his destiny? How indeed!

4.
Preparation

O F ALL the Virginia homes Maury loved to visit, Laurel Hill near Fredericksburg was his favorite. He would never forget how welcome his Aunt Elizabeth and Uncle Edward Herndon had made him feel on his first trip to Washington and on his first leave. Now he lingered there in the summer of 1830 before setting out to see his family in Tennessee. Relatives from nearby plantations dropped in to visit whenever possible. Maury enjoyed these get-togethers most of all, especially when Ann Herndon, a distant cousin, joined them.

Auburn-haired Ann had been a girl of thirteen on

his first visit. Now she was nineteen, but still eager to hear the tales of his sea adventures. Maury, for his part, could sit all evening listening to her sing Scotch ballads . . . or all summer, for that matter. Her quiet beauty and gentle manners captivated him as no Latin *señorita* could hope to. "Gentle Nannie," he was soon calling her, for he always bestowed nicknames on those he loved. Later he would look back on those days and remember:

> my first and only love, my charming Nannie, who has blessed and who now cheers and comforts me; she too called me cousin, and lent all the enchantment of young love's dream to the word.

Maury finally left for Tennessee in August, taking John's widow and sons along for the visit. His reunion with his parents and Dick made his happiness complete that summer. But Nannie continued to occupy his thoughts. He made it a point to stop again at Laurel Hill before returning to the New York Navy Yard in September.

Then at last the time was at hand for Maury to prove himself. Like all midshipmen, he had to pass his fifth-year examination in seamanship, navigation, geometry, spherics, algebra, Spanish, and moral philosophy. Future promotions would be based on the results. To prepare for it, he was assigned in December to the midshipman's school at the New York Navy Yard. Maury went with hopes that here at last the navy would concentrate on scholarly instruction.

It did not. Instead, he found a jumble of classes with little discipline and no standard textbooks. Learning by rote was again the rule, and most of the students cared for nothing but getting by with the least work possible. His efforts to gain some useful knowledge were in vain. In the end he asked for, and was granted, a leave to study on his own.

Back to Washington he journeyed, to the home of Richard B. Maury for the rest of the winter. Now he could apply himself without interruption. If his success in the navy depended upon this test, then he would be the best-prepared candidate the navy had ever known.

Word of his efforts soon circulated among other midshipmen who were in Washington for the exam. Several asked him for help in learning to solve the difficult navigation problems. He gladly drilled them in the basic rules of Bowditch, knowing they could get by with this, even though they might not understand the principles behind them.

March 3, 1831 was the date set for him to appear before the Examination Board. He went with a firm confidence and self-assurance that would soon mark all of his work. Anyone could memorize rules, but he had also mastered the theories upon which they were based. He was ready for anything the Board might ask him.

The Examination Board consisted of several old-line officers and a professor of mathematics who conducted the quizzing of the candidates. All went well with Maury until he was given the important "lunar problem" to solve. This was the method of finding longitude without using a chronometer. He could have parroted Bowditch's rules for using lunar observations like any other midshipman. But Maury was determined to show the Board the depth of his understanding. He therefore stepped to the blackboard and proceeded to work out the problem using spherical trigonometry. The professor looked on in complete bewilderment. Even more baffled were the officers. They turned to the professor for the final verdict. Rather than admit his ignorance, he promptly declared the brash young officer's solution to be wrong.

Maury was struck dumb. Could he have made a mistake? He carefully repeated the steps of his solution — with the same results. Still wrong, insisted the professor. But Maury disagreed, and at length the Board retired to make its decision.

Who was right, the determined midshipman or the equally firm professor? The Board recognized Maury's originality, but there was really no question in their minds. When it came to a dispute between a teacher and a student, they had no choice but to back the professor. They advised a stunned Maury that he had better return to sea and study his profession!

Still he somehow passed the examination. The final results placed him twenty-seventh in a class of forty — lower than any of the midshipmen he had

tutored! It would mean a delay of at least two years before his name would come up for promotion to lieutenant.

But for the moment, Passed Midshipman Maury was free to return to Laurel Hill and Nannie. They became engaged at once. Unfortunately, marriage was out of the question for a young man with no money and several years of sea duty ahead. But before he left for New York, Maury gave Nannie a token of his love: an engraved seal for sealing her letters to him. Whenever she pressed it into a drop of melted wax on an envelope flap, the word *mizpah* would appear, meaning "the Lord watch between me and thee, when we are absent one from another."

His grief of parting was somewhat soothed by the prospect of his new assignment: acting sailing master aboard the sloop-of-war *Falmouth* bound for duty with the Pacific Squadron. He would be the chief navigation officer in charge of working out latitude and longitude, as well as directing the helmsman on the proper course to steer. It was the perfect opportunity for putting his theories to practical use. But before starting out, he was again determined to prepare himself as completely as possible.

He wanted to know all there was to know about the winds and currents, tides and temperatures along the route he would be following. Well he remembered the *Brandywine*'s meandering course to Brazil and her difficulties in doubling the Horn. So many vessels followed this same track that there must be a great deal of information on hand, he reasoned. But where? He found no books on the subject in New York. Charts of the Atlantic Ocean showed nothing but latitude and longitude. Older officers shook their heads when he asked them where to locate facts on winds and currents. You learned from your superior officers on board ship. Didn't he know that the school of experience was the only method that mattered in the navy? Masters of merchant vessels glared at him suspiciously and gave him vague replies. Courses and currents were trade secrets passed from father to son among maritime men.

Yet there must be some sort of record somewhere. Of course! In the logbooks! It was all so simple once he thought of it. Every vessel afloat kept a ship's log, recording daily courses, positions, and distances. He began his search for logbooks from ships that had made the Rio–Valparaiso–Callao run. He found that he was welcome to look at any he located, but could not take them along. So he began copying extracts from every journal that recorded wind and current data. There was not much. Still, more was said about the doubling of Cape Horn than any other part of the voyage, it seemed, and he noted it carefully.

Once aboard the *Falmouth,* Maury was delighted to find himself assigned to a tiny cabin of his own. He stored his navigation books and notes in his locker, and then steeled himself for the now-familiar agony of seasickness he always suffered the first few days at sea.

As navigation officer he was not required to stand sea watches and so had much more time to himself. He used it for assembling his facts on winds and currents for the Rio passage, adding his own detailed observations as they went along. Once in port he began collecting data on the next leg of their journey by quizzing every ship's master who would tell him his experiences in rounding the Horn. Most were more than willing to give advice about this difficult passage. It had claimed more lives and caused more delays than any other stretch of water in the world. And it would remain the only western waterway into the Pacific Ocean for another eighty-three years . . . until the opening of the Panama Canal.

He was most fortunate in encountering the sealers. These hardy seamen had been hunting fur seals down among the South Shetland Islands off Antarctica and were familiar with conditions further south than most merchant or naval vessels had ever ventured. The most exciting news they imparted to Maury was the fact that winds along the Antarctic continent blew from the *east* most of the year. Just the opposite was true off Cape Horn. It was these fierce westerly gales, in fact, that caused most of the damage to shipping. Perhaps a more southerly route around the Horn was the answer. Perhaps the *Brandywine*'s quick passage in 1826, made by heading south, was more than just luck. Maury was determined to find out in the *Falmouth*.

His facts and figures on the winds and currents

around Cape Horn were much more complete than those for the Rio passage. Besides extracts from naval and merchant logbooks, he had his own notes from the *Brandywine,* as well as descriptions from sailing masters who had made the trip as many as twenty times in every season of the year.

When all were assembled before him, he was quick to note that a definite pattern emerged. Most of the ships followed one of two routes: either the inshore passage going between the islands and the coast, or the southern route staying south of the islands and Cape Horn (located on one of the islands). Quickest trips were made by inshore vessels that encountered no westerly gales. Next came those that followed the inshore route and then turned south when they met a westerly gale (as the *Brandywine* had done). Longest and most damaging of all were passages made by ships that would not abandon the inshore route despite battering storms from the west.

Maury and the *Falmouth* were put to the test in October. The British ship *Volage,* also Valparaiso-bound, sailed within hailing distance at the outset. But when both encountered fierce west winds off the Cape, the *Falmouth* turned south. Later, in his article on the navigation of Cape Horn, Maury related:

> The *Falmouth* stood down on the starboard tack to 62°5′S. and found the winds more favorable. The *Volage,* persisting in the attempt to gain the "inshore" passage, lay to on either tack, to preserve her

relative position with regard to the lat. of the Cape, and was drifted off to the eastward. When this gale abated, she stood up to the Cape again, and took another, in which she was also driven to the eastward. In the third attempt she succeeded in doubling the Cape. She put into Talcahuana, to repair the damages which she had sustained while riding out the gales from the westward. The *Falmouth* arrived in Valparaiso in excellent order.

His ship had completed the passage in twenty-four days, while the *Volage* took thirty-eight . . . a full two weeks longer. Here was more evidence to support Maury's growing conviction that a favorable route around the Horn could be charted.

It was good to be in Valparaiso again. He enjoyed riding along the hard sand beach out to the beautiful Almendral Park at the lower end of the harbor, or through the town's winding streets lined with tile-roofed houses. Stationed at every corner was one of the colorful *vigilantes,* the Chilean mounted police. With swords at their sides and lassos over their pommels, they stood ready to catch any sailor reckless enough to race his horse on a city street. Horseback riding up to the high plateau behind the city was a favorite sailor's pastime.

In the months that followed, Maury often had time to relax while his ship was anchored at Valparaiso or Callao or Guayaquil. He used it to sort through and mull over his pile of notes about the Cape Horn passage. Here in one hand he held the experience of scores of men and ships over dozens of years. Why should he be the only one to benefit from this knowledge? He decided to try his hand at turning the accumulation into some sort of essay. Writing came easy to Maury, and it would give him great satisfaction to turn out something useful for others. This was, in fact, one of the great goals in his life, for as he later remarked, "it was the aim at which all my energies were directed to make myself a useful man. I soon found that occupation, for some useful end or other, was the true secret of happiness."

But two long years of continuous duty up and down the west coast of South America took their toll on his good spirits. Nannie's letetrs were often months in reaching him. His promotion seemed more distant than ever. And home was at the other end of the earth. In 1833 Maury was twenty-seven and had served eight years in the Navy. Yet his salary was only seven hundred dollars a year. He was beginning to despair that he could ever save enough money to get married. In a letter to his brother Dick he confided:

> When I was last in the U.S., I thought if I could get employment as a surveyor, or anything of that sort, by a State, I would try a hand at it and let "Uncle Sam off"; but I believe I have too many notions, and that after all "Uncle Sam" will have the selling of my bones to the doctors.

It was his "notions" that kept him going for the

remainder of that long tour of duty. Never one to waste a spare moment, Maury began to make plans and jot down notes for another undertaking: the writing of a textbook on navigation for midshipmen. Why not? He knew the weaknesses of Bowditch firsthand. He was closer to the daily problems of midshipmen than some retired captain off in a room far from the sea. And besides, Maury enjoyed expressing himself in written words. Perhaps nothing would come of it, but at least he would make the attempt to present the theories as well as the rules of navigation in terms any midshipman could understand.

Finally in October 1833 he was transferred to the frigate *Potomac,* due to return to the States in the spring. He was prepared. Already two of his "notions" had taken on solid form: his textbook was begun, and his notes on doubling the Horn were now a complete ten-page essay. The only other matter of unfinished business was his prospective marriage to Nannie. And for that too he was prepared, enough money or not!

5.
A Crippling Blow

THEY WERE married July 15, 1834, beneath the shimmering candlelight of the great chandelier at Laurel Hill, twenty-eight-year-old Matthew Maury and his radiant Nannie. Relatives gathered to wish them well, and the exuberant Maury handed the minister his last twenty dollars.

Maury was now on a half-salary of forty dollars a month — that of a naval officer on leave and awaiting orders. Nannie, who had been living with an aunt since the death of her parents, had no money of her own. Still, their life together started on a heartening note, for Maury's first article appeared in print the very same month as their marriage.

He had submitted "On the Navigation of Cape Horn" to Yale professor Benjamin Silliman, editor of the outstanding *American Journal of Science and Arts*. Professor Silliman was greatly impressed with the young officer's collection and presentation of facts. He urged Maury to continue work on his navigation textbook.

The newlyweds chose Fredericksburg as their home while Maury awaited his next assignment. Shipboard berths were often in short supply for officers of the little American navy. Because of the few vessels on active duty, a midshipman like Maury who had just completed a long sea tour might have to remain ashore for several years.

He could have supplemented his meager salary with any sort of paid employment, just as other officers on "waiting orders" were doing. Maury decided instead to finish his textbook. To his relatives that was hardly the practical course to take. But to Maury, his only direction would always be the one which put his accumulated knowledge to a practical use. At the moment, he could not rest until he had done his bit toward improving the teaching of navigation.

Through the winter of 1834–35 he struggled along on the text and its 174 tables. By April it was finished, and he sent it to the Philadelphia publishers Key and Biddle. They accepted the manuscript immediately, to his great delight, and promised to send him proofs. He proudly dubbed it his "first-born." But on June 25 his real first-born arrived — a daughter Elizabeth, called Betty — and he was just as delighted.

This prompted the Maurys to move to more spacious quarters than the rented rooms they now occupied. They invited Nannie's younger sister and brother as well as John's widow and two boys to share with them a rented two-story house in the middle of town. Maury felt a strong sense of responsibility toward these fatherless relatives, and his sister-in-law's navy pension would add to the support of the household.

He spent the summer getting settled and awaiting his proofs. When none had arrived by October, Maury set out for Philadelphia by stagecoach to discover the reason for the delay. He found that the proofs would not be ready for another month. He decided to remain in Philadelphia until then, and rented a tiny attic room where he lived on cheese and crackers.

Back in Fredericksburg in December, he set to work on the proofreading. It was soon finished and again he had time on his hands. With no navy orders forthcoming, Maury began to look around town for something to do. One matter that promptly aroused his interest was an attempt at mining gold and iron in the surrounding countryside. This seemed an ideal time to pursue the subject, and he went about it with his usual thorough preparation, reading every book on geology and mineralogy available in Fredericksburg.

Then in April 1836 his own book appeared: *A New Theoretical and Practical Treatise on Navigation* by M. F. Maury, Passed Midshipman, United States Navy. It attracted a great deal of attention in both the United States and England. Opinions were varied. Some were shocked that a mere midshipman would be so bold as to write such a book. Certain officers belittled his efforts because of personal jealousy. But by and large the reaction was favorable. Navy professors of mathematics, whose job it was to instruct the midshipmen, were delighted to have such a practical, readable textbook at last. By 1837 a copy was ordered placed aboard every national vessel. Even Edgar Allan Poe came out with a glowing review of it in the *Southern Literary Messenger* magazine. Likewise Benjamin Silliman, to whom the book was dedicated, praised it highly. All who read it had to agree that Maury's easy, flowing style and vivid manner of expression were far superior to the dry treatment such a subject usually received.

Yet his usefulness as a midshipman was now seriously impaired. Being a successful author of a textbook for midshipmen, Midshipman Maury found himself in an awkward position. His name was still low on the promotions list and likely, under ordinary circumstances, to remain there. In a letter to Dick, Maury confided:

. . . I will let you into the secret of my plans, which I wish you to preserve as a secret, in order that, if I should not succeed in what I undertake, my friends and family may not feel the effects of disappointment. You must bear in mind that this is the first nautical work of science that has ever come from the pen of a naval officer, and upon its merits I intend to base a claim for promotion. Such a case has no precedent. Therefore you must look upon it as an experiment in which I may, or I may not, be successful. If I succeed, I shall be put over the heads of many who are now above me . . . [who] would, if they knew I contemplated such a thing, use every exertion to prevent it.

Money and position were never Maury's primary concern, but a growing family could hardly live comfortably on the salary of a midshipman. Secretary of the Navy Mahlon Dickerson thought otherwise, however, and flatly refused his personal bid for advancement in May. Later he must have had second thoughts, for on June 21 Maury's long-awaited promotion to lieutenant actually came through. No doubt many of his fellow officers felt he deserved it, but there were others who bitterly resented his rise in rank, as they had been passed over.

Meanwhile, Maury's new interest in the field of geology led him to accept the position of superintendent at a nearby gold mine for the summer. The owner was so pleased with his work that he urged him to consider a permanent appointment. But the low-yield ore and the small-scale operation offered little challenge for Maury's full energies. He wrote one paper on the subject and invented a new process for eliminating waste. Then in September he turned again to the navy, determined to get back into active duty. His timing was right but his move unfortunate, for it embroiled Maury in a political controversy which would haunt him for years to come.

In the spring of 1836 Congress had authorized the budding United States Navy to undertake its first exploring expedition: to the southern Pacific Ocean. President Andrew Jackson wholeheartedly supported the operation. It was Secretary Dickerson who, strangely enough, stirred up most of the opposition. The President appointed Commodore Thomas Jones as leader of the expedition, and Jones began by selecting commanders for the two vessels under him. Almost at once Secretary Dickerson interfered, trying to get his own man, Charles Wilkes, appointed.

Even Maury's name came up for commander, backed by his former teacher James Otey, now the Right Reverend James Otey, Episcopal Bishop of Tennessee. Maury knew nothing would come of it because of his earlier encounter with the Secretary. Instead, he was pleased to accept the post of first officer aboard one of the vessels.

The expedition was scheduled to depart from Norfolk in the fall. But political bickering in Washington caused delay after delay, until another spring rolled around with Maury still land-locked. He was beginning to wonder about the wisdom of being involved in such an unpromising affair, when a letter from the Secretary arrived, ordering him to report for regular duty aboard the frigate *Macedonian*! Either Dickerson had forgotten about Maury's expedition post, or he now wanted him out of it. In the end the disgruntled young officer rejected both positions and asked for an extension on his leave.

It was a poor time to turn down active duty with its increased pay, for his second child, Diana, was born June 25, 1837. He nicknamed her "Nannie Curly" and thereafter called his wife "Nan."

Surprisingly, Maury's move proved to his advantage, for he was next offered the post of expedition astronomer. This he gladly accepted, and departed at once for Philadelphia to prepare himself.

Then in November, Commodore Jones sent him to Washington on a seemingly simple mission: to collect the expedition's newly purchased navigation instruments. But Charles Wilkes, head of the Depot of Charts and Instruments, gave him few instruments and much trouble. The ill-starred expedition was far too embroiled in personal jealousies and political intrigues for Maury to save. In the end Commodore Jones himself, along with most of his appointees, resigned from the expedition in disgust. When Wilkes was appointed to take over, Maury felt he had no choice but to turn in his own resignation. Once afloat, the Wilkes South Sea Exploring Expedition proved its worth, but the ill will it had created among all those involved remained a sore spot in the navy for many years.

To Maury it meant two good years of his life gone for nothing. Was this to be the pattern of his naval career? There must be a better way to run a national department, he reasoned. Almost always when Maury was at his lowest ebb like this, he turned to writing: letters, articles, or just ideas jotted down on paper. Now it took the form of five newspaper articles criticizing Dickerson's blundering and calling for improvement on the part of the newly appointed Secretary James K. Paulding. The pieces appeared in the Richmond, Virginia *Whig and Public Advertiser* under the pen name of Harry Bluff. Such interest was aroused that he continued the series under the pen name of Will Watch, with seven more articles answering questions raised by Harry Bluff. Maury's own identity was carefully guarded, and most readers thought that the author was a prominent captain.

Finally, in December 1838 Maury received orders to report to Washington for active duty under Lieutenant James Glynn on the little steamer *Engineer*. They were to survey harbors in North and South Carolina and Georgia to determine the best location for a new naval yard. Glynn was another of the expedition officers who had resigned. Now the two of them made the best of this rather routine duty. It was a far cry from exploring the South Seas or charting a Cape Horn passage. Yet hydrography itself, the science of measuring and mapping areas of water, held great appeal for Maury. If only their mission were more challenging!

It was a relief to return to Fredericksburg in the summer of 1839 after the survey was completed. Maury was to exchange his little steamer for the larger brig *Consort,* due to depart from New York in October. Until then he was free. After a short rest at home, he decided to visit his parents in Tennessee. They were getting too old to handle the farm, and he hoped to arrange for them to live elsewhere. He was able to see them off to his sister Betsy's home, thirty-five miles down the Mississippi from Memphis. Then he started on the long haul back to New York and his ship.

Roads were much improved since his first Tennessee trip fourteen years earlier. Stagecoach lines now took great pride in transporting their passengers over the many new turnpikes in record time. Still it was a long and tiresome trip. By October 17 Maury was on one of the swift night stages which would whisk him through Ohio to Wheeling, then into Virginia. He had been dozing, but awoke at Lancaster when three more passengers entered the already full coach. One was a woman, and Maury, with his typical Southern gallantry, offered her his seat while he climbed up beside the driver.

For a while Maury enjoyed the brisk night air, but the coach now swayed from side to side even more violently than usual. Extra baggage and passengers had made it somewhat topheavy. About an hour out of Somerset, Ohio, they reached a blockade where the turnpike was being repaired and were forced to take a detour. Now the overloading of the stage was even more evident in the soft tracks of the newly made road. Even the driver commented on it. Hardly had the words been spoken when the stage gave a sudden lurch to the right and overturned. Maury was dashed to the ground with a bone-crunching jolt. He sat up immediately, but the pain in his

right leg was so intense that he nearly fainted.

He knew at once that the injury was serious, and refused to let the driver move him. One of the passengers returned to Somerset by horseback for a doctor. Maury lay in agony until the doctor's arrival at dawn in another stagecoach. It was decided that he must be carried back to Somerset, although the town had no hospital but only a little inn called the Phoenix Tavern. There the doctor did his best to repair the ruined leg. He found that the thigh bone and kneepan were both badly fractured, and that the knee joint itself was dislocated and the ligaments torn.

Although the doctor was able to get the swollen joint back into place, he made a bad job of setting

the thigh bone and it had to be redone — all without an anaesthetic. Yet it was not the searing pain that bothered Maury so, but the haunting fear that he might never walk again. What good was a naval officer with a crippled leg?

6.
The Lucky Bag

FOR WEEKS Maury lay in his dingy little inn room, unable to move without excruciating pains shooting up and down his leg, unable to be moved without permanent damage to the limb. The owner of the tavern and his sharp-tongued wife were no help at all. From the start they hadn't liked Maury's looks. His clothes, his manners and his Southern accent marked him for an aristocrat — probably some rich plantation owner. The sooner they got rid of him the better.

They refused to put a guard in front of his small open fireplace until the floor had caught fire three times. They grudgingly served him half-cooked food in greasy pewterware until he nearly became sick. When his doctor smuggled him a clean silver spoon, the innkeeper stopped speaking to him. Maury even found that the can he was given for making his tea doubled as his host's shaving mug! He finally hired a boy to wait on him, and they dined together on roasted apples and milk.

Nan set out for Somerset as soon as she heard the news, but took sick the first day and had to return. At last the family sent John Minor, one of the Fredericksburg relatives. John's companionship cheered Maury no end, and he soon felt well enough to fill his idle hours with something useful. He sent John eighteen miles over to Lancaster to buy a French grammar, and was soon totally immersed in learning a new language.

"I try to make the mind do something to give it the habit of obedience to the will, whenever the faculties are not sleeping," Maury wrote in one of his many letters to friends and relatives. He would never feel completely useless so long as he could learn something new. Nor would he ever be lonely so long as he could talk to his loved ones through letters.

But the leg! Although the bones would heal, torn tendons and muscles made movement of it next to impossible. Yet he hobbled about on the other leg and crutches as soon as he could stand it. By January he was able to travel home. In February, nearly five months after the accident, a doctor's examination rated him: "total disability as regards duty."

It never occurred to Maury to feel sorry for himself. Instead, he bent all his efforts toward getting back on his feet. He forced himself to exercise the crippled limb. He played and joked with the children. He made himself as busy as possible. But he could not help wondering. In a letter to a cousin, Ann Maury, he spoke of his uncertainties:

Sometimes I think — when I become desperate — that I'll write. Sometimes I have a notion to take to books and be learned; but then such vast fields and pastures and wastes and seas of unexplored knowledge appear on the horizon, my ignorance sickens at the prospect. I am reminded of how little, how very little, I do know; just enough to be sensible of this fact. Then I'll content myself with cultivating a few little patches of knowledge. What shall they be? Shall they be light or heat? — storms or currents? — ship-building or ship-sailing? — steam or trajectiles? — hollow shot or gravitation? — gases or fluids? — winds or tides? — or —— And in the wilderness of subjects, the mind is confused and knows not which to choose; so I play with the children and bend the knee, which, though now more readily bent, does not admit of but very little more flexion than it did when I saw you.

By March he felt well enough to request a naval assignment that could be performed on crutches. None was forthcoming. He hardly expected it would be. The Navy Department was becoming more inefficient and unreliable every year! It saddened his heart to see how low his chosen profession had fallen since the glorious days of his brother's career during the War of 1812. Now in the 1840s the older American naval officers were often embarrassed in foreign ports because their highest rank was only captain. They were ridiculed at home because few had any formal training other than that on shipboard. While France and England had already begun converting to steam, America's ocean-going vessels were all sailing ships — and old ones at that. It was high time for a change.

Maury had often discussed the subject with fellow officers. They might differ about what should be done, but all agreed it *was* time for a change. Suddenly Maury realized he was now in a position to do something about it. With all the time in the world on his hands, he decided to pick up his pen again and finish what he had started in 1838 with his Harry Bluff and Will Watch articles.

This new series he would call "Scraps from the Lucky Bag." No navy man could miss the point. All knew that almost any item might be pulled from a lucky bag, bringing swift discipline to its luckless owner. Maury arranged to have the articles published in the prominent *Southern Literary Messenger.* They would deal with topics such as new ranks for naval officers, adoption of steam power, supplying ships at half the usual cost, and establishing a school for midshipmen. He would also discuss using rifle guns and hollow shot in what he called "a new era in naval warfare, that of big guns and small ships." At a time when some frigates carried as many as 120 guns, his vision that ships might one day need only half a dozen was farsighted indeed. He kept the pen name Harry Bluff, so there was still great speculation over the author's identity.

His "little patches of knowledge" covered ground seldom trod before. He was among the first advocates of "great circle sailing" to shorten the distance between America and England. He argued that sailing a straight line as plotted across a flat chart was not the shortest route between two points on the round earth.

The Gulf Stream and its causes also intrigued him. His "lucky bag" was, in fact, overflowing both with ideas and with constructive criticism. It was the perfect outlet for his pent-up energy, and he was free to say what he liked. When and if the Navy Department discovered that Harry Bluff was Matthew Maury, what could it do? Many officers would congratulate him for alerting the public. Those who might object were no threat to him. After all, what could they do to make him worse off than he was already?

Reaction to "Scraps" was much as he had expected. Many were relieved to have the problems aired in print. A few were infuriated. But Maury was only more restless than ever to get back on his feet. Writing would never exhaust the total energy of this man of action. Exercising his leg helped somewhat, but the slowness of its healing tried his patience. "The leg gains strength slowly," he wrote to his parents. "I can walk now with the assistance of a stick only; but a walk of two or three hundred yards breaks me down. A terrible calamity is this, indeed, to me."

Then in late August he received orders to report to Washington for a complete examination by navy surgeons. Maury was elated. He stopped by to see the new Navy Secretary and extracted the promise of an assignment on the hydrographic vessel still surveying harbors in South Carolina. Then he visited the doctors. Their opinion was just as gloomy as his own private physician's. They rated him at "three-fourths a degree of total permanent disability." The navy had no use for such a man, so Maury took up his pen again. Nan was his only ray of hope that fall. On October 9 she bore him his first son, Richard Launcelot, named after his brother and of course called "Dick."

Then in late winter, the spark ignited by his lucky-bag articles really caught fire. In exposing certain graft connected with shipbuilding and supplying, he accidentally exposed his own identity. The Navy Board of Commissioners raised a great hue and cry, denying everything and publishing its own views. Soon reporters were hot on his trail, and newspapers up and down the country were ringing with the navy scandal. In the end they proposed Maury for the new Secretary of the Navy. Since only a civilian could occupy this post, they suggested he resign his naval commission at once, so that President John Tyler could make the appointment.

Maury was much annoyed. Nothing could be further from his desire — he had no wish to be Secretary of the Navy. He had no intention of resigning from his chosen field. All he really wanted was to be put back on active duty — back on board a ship, or at some responsible nautical post on shore.

There is no doubt that Maury was a thorn in the side of the Navy Department. What were they to do with him? A midshipman who published works on navigation . . . a lieutenant who pointed up the navy's weaknesses so forcefully . . . a brilliant young officer with so much to offer . . . and yet a cripple!

At first the answer seemed to lie in Commodore Thomas Jones's offer of a flag lieutenant's berth on the flagship of the Pacific Squadron. He was more than willing to have Maury, cripple or not.

Maury jumped at the chance, and immediately informed the Secretary of his willingness. Nan and his Fredericksburg friends were appalled. Didn't he realize how little his leg had healed? How quickly he grew tired? How greatly his health had suffered? The exertions of sea duty might kill him, or at the very least cripple him permanently. Secretly they requested three of the community's leading doctors to inform the Navy Secretary of Maury's true condition and his total unfitness for sea duty on a man-of-war.

When this blow fell, Maury accepted it as best he could and turned again to his writing. Meanwhile, fellow officers who were anxious to see him back on active duty suggested that he might head a new hydrographical bureau soon to be set up. Land duty was far inferior to sea duty by any navy man's standard — even the pay was lower — but Maury had little choice. Still, he showed no interest in it until he heard it might go to a civilian because no navy officer was qualified. This was all the challenge Maury needed.

In the end the hydrographical bureau remained on paper, while Maury was called upon to head its forerunner, the dingy little Depot of Charts and Instruments — Charles Wilkes's old job. It was a poor substitute for navigating a ship or charting unknown seas. Yet Maury never realized, as he packed his bag for Washington, that the job itself hardly mattered. He had it within him to make any task he attempted an extraordinary one.

In July of 1842 the entire Depot of Charts and Instruments was housed in two rooms of Wilkes's Washington home. The day Matthew Maury limped through its door he unknowingly entered his life's great work.

7.
The Depot

MAURY'S first undertaking in Washington was to remove the Depot to new premises. Wilkes would be returning soon from his South Sea expedition and wanting his old quarters back. So Maury went house hunting. It was no easy task in 1842. The Nation's capital was still a hodgepodge of unfinished buildings, unpaved streets, and mud holes. Hogs wallowed under the trees along Pennsylvania Avenue, the main thoroughfare. Trains chugged across the weed-choked Mall to the Baltimore & Ohio Railroad station on a corner of the Capitol grounds. The Capitol itself stood without its dome in a welter of scaffolding and braces. At the opposite end of the Mall rose the stump of the Washington Monument like a broken chimney in a cow pasture. The most imposing buildings in town were the white marble Patent Office and the Greek-columned Post Office across from it. Even the White House was a plain structure surrounded by a vegetable garden.

At last Maury located a suitable house at 2422–2424 Pennsylvania Avenue, and began the transfer of records and equipment. There were quadrants, sextants, barometers, and chronometers, all stored in the Depot at the end of every ship's voyage. There was the large telescope used for observing the transit of heavenly bodies across the Washington meridian to determine exact time. There were rolls and rolls of musty old charts for every harbor and sea in the world. And there were logbooks — piles of dusty, moldering old ships' logs, accumulated since the Depot's founding in 1830.

From the beginning it was obvious to Maury what his main task must be. One look at the outdated charts told him. Some were over one hundred years old. Most had been made and purchased in foreign countries. All had great blank spaces where water depths and coastlines were unknown. None had anything at all to say about winds and currents, the principal concern of navigators.

He gathered his staff together (four lieutenants, eight passed midshipmen, one clerk, and one draftsman) and outlined their duties. They were to go through every one of the old logbooks, extracting every scrap of information on force of winds, set of currents, temperature of the sea, lengths of daily runs, compass bearings, weather . . . anything and everything that might assist a navigator. It was Maury's intention to redo the charts, making them more complete and accurate and helpful to mariners than anything that had ever been done before.

Why not? He knew just what a navigator needed, having been one himself. He knew exactly where to find the information, having searched long and hard for it. And now he was in charge of the very office whose duty it was to supply such charts. He had no intention of buying them from Europe as his predecessors had done. Not when the prime source of all navigational experience stood stacked before him in every nook and cranny of his new house. The logbooks! Thousands of them! A veritable bonanza!

His staff must have looked with dismay at this strange, forceful little man with the pronounced limp and the twinkling blue eyes. At thirty-six Maury was short and stocky with a massive head of wavy brown hair, delicate hands that gestured as he spoke, and clear, intelligent eyes that seemed to see value in the most unlikely objects. His staff shook their heads over the moldy old logs. Besides their many regular duties, they would have to read through all of these? Surely he couldn't be serious!

But his enthusiasm was contagious, and eventually everyone pitched in with a will. They began by dividing the books according to geographical regions. There were more records of the New York–Rio de Janeiro run than any other. Then the really time-consuming reading began. Day after day the midshipmen pored over the fading scripts.

As facts emerged, Maury sorted and sifted and arranged them on paper or scratched them across old charts. It was just as it had been on the Cape Horn passage. The logs revealed well-defined routes across the sea, taking advantage of helpful winds and currents and avoiding contrary ones. Yet these were not the routes most captains sailed. Instead of putting natural conditions to work for them, tradition-bound mariners were going hundreds of miles out of their way to avoid them, it seemed to Maury. If only they had his facts at their disposal, they could find and follow the natural "paths" through the sea. And what a boon for the beginning navigator, he thought, recalling his *Falmouth* experience. After careful consideration, he decided to begin with the Atlantic Ocean, constructing his new charts thus (as he later wrote in his *Physical Geography of the Sea*):

> By putting down on a chart the tracks of many vessels on the same voyage, but at different times, in different years, and during all seasons, and by projecting along each track the winds and currents daily encountered, it was plain that navigators hereafter, by consulting this chart, would have for their guide the results of the combined experience of all whose tracks were thus pointed out. . . . All this

could be taken in at a glance, and thus the young mariner, instead of groping his way along until the lights of experience should come to him by the slow teachings of the dearest of all schools, would here find, at once, that he had already the experience of a thousand navigators to guide him on his voyage.

But the logbooks were not enough. Too many captains had been skimpy with the data they were supposed to record. Maury finally convinced his superiors to order captains now at sea to send him more detailed information. Facts trickled in as the months passed by, but not fast enough nor complete enough to suit Maury. So he devised an abstract log to be carried by all public cruisers, filled in, and returned to the Depot. There were spaces for recording latitude, longitude, magnetic variation, wind direction and rate, barometer height, current direction and rate, temperature of air, temperature of water at surface and depth, cloud forms and direction . . . and all to be taken several times a day. Most navy captains, already overburdened, got by with as little of this recording as possible. So Maury's charts progressed slowly.

Not so his regular chores. He kept the Depot of Charts and Instruments humming with activity. Besides the normal checking and rating of instruments, observing star transits, making mathematical computations, keeping records and compiling data, he even managed to put out a weekly weather journal.

In the evening he intensified his studies on all manner of subjects important to his work. The Gulf Stream occupied much of his thought for many months in 1844. The scientific paper he prepared on it became the main speech of the day at a meeting of the National Institute in Washington. All of this studying and writing he did in the family parlor, to the delight of his children, and not even the youngest (two-year-old John, born in 1842) could bother him. His years in the noisy steerage had inured him to any distraction. One of his daughters, Diana Maury Corbin, later recalled:

> Sometimes he would walk up and down the two parlours wrapped in a light blue silk Japanese dressing-gown, . . . the long ribbons, which should have been fastened around his waist, trailing behind him, or gathered up like reins in the hands of one of the little ones, who trotted after him, backwards and forwards, calling out "Gee, woa!" or "Back, sir!" — he paying not the slightest attention, but dictating gravely.

Meanwhile, the navy's expanded scientific work did not go unnoticed. Congress at last voted funds for a permanent building to house the Depot as well as a national observatory. The Secretary of the Navy then sent Lieutenant James M. Gillis to Europe to purchase telescopes for the observatory.

As work began on the building, there was great speculation in Washington over who would be appointed to head the new United States Naval Observatory and Hydrographical Office. Would it be Lieutenant Maury, a competent head of the Depot of Charts and Instruments, but with little formal training in astronomy? Would it be Lieutenant Gillis, a trained astronomer as well as a former head of the Depot? Or would it be a civilian scientist?

Opinion leaned first one way and then another during the summer of 1844. It made Maury bristle to hear once again how many people thought the navy had no one qualified to handle such a post. He knew the work would be similar to that which he himself was successfully handling at the Depot. As for Lieutenant Gillis, Maury had to admit that he too was qualified, especially as an astronomer. But if Gillis held the post, what would become of the new charts?

Gillis himself believed he deserved the post. After all, he had just selected and purchased the instruments for it. Moreover, he had the backing of the two most important men of science in Washington: Professor Joseph Henry, Secretary of the Smithsonian Institution, and Professor Alexander Dallas Bache, Superintendent of the United States Coast Survey and great-grandson of Benjamin Franklin. Both Henry and Bache would sanction only a formally trained scientist like Gillis. Besides, Bache would never support a rival like Maury . . . a man who specialized in chartmaking and therefore threatened the Coast Survey . . . a man who dared to pose as an authority on the Gulf Stream, the Franklin family's own special field!

Yet September started on a bright note for Maury. His navigation textbook was formally designated as the chief text for midshipmen. Those who doubted his ability had only to leaf through its pages. Perhaps there was never any doubt in the mind of the Secretary of the Navy. On October 1, 1844, he appointed Matthew Maury Superintendent of the United States Naval Observatory and Hydrographical Office.

Maury commented in a letter to a friend: "I have solved a problem that has often blistered my heart, and proved that Navy officers are fit for something else than scrubbing decks at sea and tacking ship"

He accepted the post with pleasure, but with it came three more enemies.

8.
The Observatory

Now that he was officially the Superintendent, Maury looked over the brand-new Observatory building more carefully. It stood on Camp Hill, a hundred-foot rise above the Potomac River about a mile west of the White House. Between the hill and the river lay acres of marshy flats, rather wild but not unpleasant to look at, Maury noted. He might have changed his opinion had he known about the malaria-carrying mosquitos which would drive him out of Washington every summer for years to come.

The building itself was a red brick square of two

stories, with a one-story wing at the right and the left. Later the Superintendent's residence would be added to the left wing. Over the central portion rose a twenty-three-foot copper dome mounted on revolving cannon balls. It stood above the navy's best telescope, the 9.6-inch Equatorial Refractor. Also in the Equatorial room was a smaller comet seeker with a four-inch glass.

Downstairs in the east wing was the five-foot Mural Circle with its 4.1-inch telescope. This was the principal instrument for determining a star's "declination," or latitude in the sky. In the west

wing stood the Prime Vertical Transit instrument with its 4.9-inch glass. This telescope was used to observe the passage, or "transit," of a heavenly body over the Washington meridian, the imaginary line from the North Pole to the South Pole which passed through Washington, D.C.

Maury knew that the main objective of all observations with any of his instruments would be the same as it had been at the Depot: to determine time, the most accurate time possible, according to the stars as well as the sun. A ship's exact position at sea could be calculated only when a navigator knew the correct time down to the fraction of a second. An error of only four seconds meant an error of a whole degree in longitude (60 nautical miles). Time on board ship was kept by boxed clocks called chronometers. It was Maury's job to check these instruments regularly against his main clock in Washington. This clock's time was regulated entirely by transits of the sun and moon, of the planets Mars, Venus, Saturn, and Jupiter, and of the principal stars.

Above and beyond this task, the new Observatory's primary role in American astronomy was entirely up to its Superintendent. After considering a number of possibilities, Maury finally settled on a grand scheme: to catalogue the entire heavens visible from Washington. As noted in an article about the new Observatory in an 1899 issue of *Science* magazine, Maury had proposed:

> . . . a regular and systematic exploration of the whole heavens from 45° south . . . with the intention of penetrating with the telescope every point of space from that parallel of declination up to the north pole, and of assigning position to every star, down to the 10th magnitude, that shall pass through the field of view.

No one in the United States had attempted such an ambitious survey before, and it was just the sort of impossible project that appealed to Maury. "How far we shall fall short of it remains for results to show," he had added.

At once he began to train his three lieutenants

and six passed midshipmen so that every telescope would have at least two observers. But Maury himself was the principal user of the Equatorial for the first two years. There was something about looking into the star-filled heavens that affected him as deeply as anything he would ever witness on earth. Perhaps he felt the hand of God moving more directly there than anywhere else, for Maury was a profoundly religious man. Whenever he talked about watching stars through the telescope he did so most vividly: — for example, in an address he made in 1855 before the literary societies of the University of Virginia:

> . . . of all the wonders and beauties that are revealed by this instrument, the simple passage of a star across the meridian is to me the most grand and imposing. . . . At the dead of night, when the noise of the city is hushed in sleep, and all is still, I sometimes go over alone to the Observatory to revel in this glorious spectacle. The assistants, wearied with watching, have retired to rest, and there is not a sound to be heard in the building save the deadbeat escapement of the clock, telling the footsteps of time in his ceaseless round. I take up the Ephemeris [astronomical almanac], and find, by calculation made years ago, that a star which I have never seen will, when the hand of that clock points to a certain instant of time, enter the field of the telescope, flit across the meridian and disappear. The instrument is set, and as the moment draws near, the stillness becomes more and more impressive. . . .

A pure bright star is marching through the field to the music of the spheres; and at the very instant predicted, even to the fraction of a second, it stalks across the wire and is gone. The song that was sung by the morning stars has been felt, and the heart, swelling with emotions too deep for the organs of speech, almost bursts with the unutterable anthem.

Maury's background for this sort of work was limited to the training he had undertaken in Philadelphia in 1837 as appointed astronomer to the South Sea Exploring Expedition, in addition to the nautical astronomy he had learned aboard ship. Now he pored over the works of modern European astronomers to absorb anything new in the field. The Frenchman Pierre-Simon de Laplace had set the stage for astronomy in the nineteenth century with his discoveries of the principles behind the movements of heavenly bodies. Previously, it was possible for man to fear that the moon might suddenly crash into the earth or a planet like Venus fly off into space. Now astronomers around the world were busily applying Laplace's "law of universal attraction" to their own studies of the heavens.

Maury's first volume on astronomical observations came out in 1846, immediately establishing the United States Naval Observatory on a par with those in Europe. Again there were people who expressed surprise that a naval officer had done it.

The new year had started out on another bright note as well, with Maury witnessing a startling phenomenon. All the world had been fascinated by Biela's comet since its appearance the previous November. This was one of the comets which returned to earth periodically. On the night of January 13, as Maury followed its progress across the sky, he suddenly saw the fiery ball split completely in two and continue on. Maury described the extraordinary experience in another well-received scientific paper.

But as the year continued new problems arose. In February an able and experienced civilian astronomer, Sears Walker, was assigned to the Observatory. From the start there was trouble. Walker was not used to navy ways. Moreover, he considered Maury and his staff mere amateurs in the field of astronomy. He refused to let himself be charmed by Maury's personal magnetism as the others seemed to be. In short, Walker refused to follow orders, and would apply himself only to work that interested him. Maury tried to make the best of the situation, for Walker was an excellent computer.

To make matters more complicated, war was declared against Mexico in the spring. Immediately Maury offered his services and those of his junior officers wherever they might be needed. The navy accepted several of the younger men but left Maury at his post, much to his disappointment. The thick of battle was the only place for a navy officer when his country was at war, he believed. Again and again as the war progressed, Maury offered his services — only to be turned down. His game leg and his vital duties ashore kept him out of the action.

At home things were more cheerful. Warm-hearted Maury was always at his best in the midst of his family. He especially enjoyed talking and playing with the children. His fifth child, Mary (called "Tots"), had been born the previous autumn, and this made quite a houseful, including the cousins.

A typical day started with his shaving ritual. The whole tribe was in on it. The youngest sat on the bureau holding his soap. The rest stood on either side like doctors' assistants. One held the razor, one the brush, one a towel, and the others, papers for wiping the razor. Maury would stir his water, mumbling as it heated, "Double, double, toil and trouble, fire burn and cauldron bubble," like the witches in Shakespeare's *Macbeth*. Then he would tell them adventurous stories of his Tennessee boyhood until they knew them all by heart.

He spent as much time as possible with his children, often taking them for long walks to observe nature. Occasionally he even allowed them to look at the stars through the Equatorial telescope at the Observatory.

He did not believe in punishing children except for lying or disobedience. Even then he was not harsh, but very swift and effective, as Nannie Curly had occasion to learn to her everlasting regret. She had early expressed a love for natural history, encouraged by her father. Then one day an instrument maker sent Maury a brass-mounted telescope. He told Nannie it would be hers when she had learned to handle the big telescope at the Observatory and when she could find any star by obtaining its right ascension (heavenly longitude) and declination (heavenly latitude) from the Nautical Almanac.

She learned how in less than a month, and the glorious prize was hers. Thereafter, she spent long hours star-gazing, even in the daytime with a colored lens attached, when she should have been doing her chores. Finally Maury had to speak to her because she had neglected some necessary mending. He gave her an hour and a half to complete it. Sorrowfully Nannie Curly carried the 'scope upstairs to put it away, but something made her sneak just one more look from the library window. Before she knew it, the time was up and the mending still not done. Without a word Maury packed up the telescope, and Nannie never saw it again.

At the Observatory the Mexican War continued to disrupt the regular routine. Every time a young officer became skilled at his job, he would be taken for shipboard duty. As a result Maury's star cataloguing suffered.

Then in September an event occurred which electrified the entire scientific world. A new planet was discovered entirely by calculation. Using Laplace's principles, Urbain Leverrier of France and John Couch Adams of the United States separately fixed the position of an unknown body in the solar system, and told astronomers where to look for it. On

September 23, 1846, Johann Gottfried Galle in Germany found it — the planet Neptune, as it came to be called — in the precise spot that had been predicted.

This gave Maury the idea that perhaps Neptune had already been recorded by someone else as a fixed star. He set Sears Walker to work on the monumental task of sifting through years of earlier observations from all parts of the world. After four months of determined research, Walker proved this important fact to be true. Neptune had indeed been recorded as a fixed star on May 8 and 9, 1795, in Paris. This was news the scientific world would welcome, for it was now possible to trace Neptune's orbit.

Maury was pleased to think that the United States Naval Observatory could claim credit for such an important find. But first there was the matter of Mr. Walker to settle. Relations between Walker and Maury had become increasingly difficult. When Maury learned from outside sources that Walker planned to resign soon, he confronted him openly. There was a disagreeable exchange of words. In the end Maury let him go. He was promptly hired by Professor Bache at the Coast Survey. Maury regretted the incident but thought no more about it — that is, until he received his August 1847 copy of the German journal *Astronomische Nachrichten*.

There he was astounded to read a complete description of Walker's research on the planet Neptune submitted to the magazine by none other than Joseph Henry of the Smithsonian. Maury was sure there must be some mistake. Perhaps Henry's name had been forged. After all, the head of one scientific institution did not steal data on work done in another.

Maury promptly wrote to Henry about the matter. Henry replied that Walker had personally brought him the material and asked to have it published. Furthermore, Henry criticized Maury's style of scientific correspondence, and asked him to state his complaint more explicitly. This Maury did in a longer second letter. Henry answered in a brief note that no intentional harm to the Observatory had been done. Maury then wrote a third letter asking Henry to send the German journal a statement of the Observatory's part in the research. Henry never answered.

9.
Wind and Current Charts

P ART OF the trouble lay in Maury's failure to con- fine his work to one field. Tracing winds at sea soon led him to study winds and weather on the land. But this was Professor Henry's special concern at the Smithsonian, and he would never permit Maury's interference. Charting the depths of the ocean led Maury to plot the approaches to American harbors. But this was Professor Bache's business at the Coast Survey, and he was determined to keep Maury out.

Yet Maury's universal mind refused to limit itself to a single field and he would later write in defense of this stand in *The Physical Geography of the Sea*:

Properly to appreciate the various offices which the winds and the waves perform, we must regard nature as a whole, for all the departments thereof are intimately connected. If we attempt to study in one of them, we often find ourselves tracing clews which insensibly lead us off into others, and, before we are aware, we discover ourselves exploring the chambers of some other department.

While his enemies plotted his downfall, Maury continued to pursue his studies no matter where they led him, so long as they promised to benefit mankind.

By the late 1840s his main concern was the new charts. The long hours of work by his hard-pressed staff had finally borne results. Maury had enough information from logbooks to plot the entire Atlantic Ocean. First he divided the area into squares of 5° to a side and drew a compass in the middle of each. Next he sifted through the data and wrote down in each square the total number of observations made in that particular spot, as well as the percentage of calm days found there. Then on each of the compass's sixteen directional points in each square, he wrote the percentage of winds found to blow from that quarter and the percentage of miles a ship would lose in sailing through that square in that particular direction. It was then up to the navigator to determine which squares would take him where he was going most efficiently.

His findings were revolutionary. For example, the

winds and currents off Cape San Roque, Brazil, were found not to be dangerous, despite centuries of tradition to the contrary. Therefore, Maury advised Rio-bound mariners to stay close to the Cape in his *Explanations and Sailing Directions to Accompany the Wind and Current Charts.*

Showing a captain the best course to take was one thing, but convincing him to take it was another matter entirely. Why should an experienced navigator abandon the safe and sure course he had always followed? How could a land-bound scientist know more than a deep-water mariner who had been sailing the course for years? And what if the chart were wrong and a vessel should break its back on the rugged Cape? Let another man try it, was the attitude of most captains. For them the old ways were still the best.

There was another man — to Maury's everlasting gratitude. Early in January 1848 a Captain Jackson, commander of the merchant bark *W. H. D. C. Wright* out of Baltimore, decided to give Maury's chart a try. The Rio run was nothing new to Jackson, for he sailed it twice a year, hauling flour south and returning with a cargo of coffee.

The usual passage took fifty-five days each way, so he was expected to be away at least four months. But this time he quickly noticed a difference. Along Maury's route the winds were fair almost every day just as predicted. Even in the doldrums there was enough of a breeze to carry him across this dreaded belt of calms. Off Cape San Roque a freshening wind actually helped him along instead of driving him to destruction on the rocks. He reached Rio in thirty-eight days, an amazing saving of seventeen days.

But just in case the whole thing had been a lucky accident, Jackson repeated the course on his return trip. It was an almost exact duplication of the outward voyage. He arrived in Baltimore in 37 days — *a total of 35 days before he was expected.* No one could believe it. Surely he hadn't really gone all the way to Rio and back! But there were his holds, full to the brim with Brazilian coffee!

The news spread like wildfire up and down the waterfront . . . by word of mouth to Philadelphia . . . by newspaper to New York and Boston. Soon captains everywhere were clamoring for Wind and Current Charts. They would pay any amount for a copy.

Maury rose to the occasion with the same originality that had marked his days since he first bargained for a horse to carry him out of the Tennessee hills. He would not sell the charts for money. They could be acquired only through the price of co-operation. A captain had to agree to fill out and return a ten-page abstract log of his voyages. It was a brilliant move, for in this manner Maury was assured a steady flow of up-to-date information for future charts.

By 1849 he had published Wind and Current Charts of the Atlantic, Pacific, and Indian Oceans, and started work on a new series which would one day become the United States Navy's famous Pilot Charts.

Merchants and shipowners of the great northeastern ports were quick to realize the value of Maury's studies. Every day of shipping saved meant a saving of hundreds of dollars to them. Shipping concerns in Boston offered to raise $50,000 to buy Maury a research vessel. He declined with thanks, explaining that it was a navy project and must use naval vessels. They then petitioned the government for a man-of-war to be put at Maury's disposal. Finally in March of 1849 Congress actually passed an act authorizing three small naval vessels to be used for oceanic researches. But knowing politics as he did, Maury was pleased to get even one of these.

Maury's charts could not have been completed at a more opportune moment, for 1849 was the year of the great gold rush to California. Speed was the thing. A fortune awaited the miner or merchant who got there first. Clipper-ship captains began relying on Maury's charts to speed them along their tricky passage around Cape Horn. For a vessel using Maury's charts, 144½ days was the average time from New York to San Francisco. Those who failed to take advantage of these guides averaged 187½ days — 43 days longer!

In 1851 the incredible *Flying Cloud* established the most amazing record of all: 89 days, 21 hours from New York to San Francisco. Her tapered, copper-sheathed hull and her billowing head of sail

swept her across the sea like no other ship on earth. But it was the Wind and Current Charts and *Sailing Directions* that showed her the shortcuts. With clipper ships like this to lead the way, even the most tradition-bound captain had to admit the charts were worth while. By the end of 1851 more than a thousand American ships carried Maury's charts and sent him their logs.

Perhaps Maury's charts were not so extraordinary — merely the assemblage of facts that had been there all along. Perhaps another man could have done the same thing, as his enemies claimed. But surely Maury's stroke of genius was enlisting the aid of ordinary mariners to contribute their bit to science. They would ever be appreciative, as Captain Phinney of the clipper *Gertrude* wrote to Maury:

> Such as it is, I am happy to contribute my mite towards furnishing you with material to work out still farther towards perfection your great and glorious task, not only of pointing out the most speedy route for ships to follow over the ocean, but also teaching us sailors to look about us and recognize the wonderful manifestations of the wisdom and goodness of the great God, by which we are constantly surrounded. For myself, I am free to confess that for many years I commanded a ship, and although never insensible of the beauties of nature upon sea and land, I yet feel, that until I took up your work I had been traversing the ocean blindfold. . . . You have taught me to look above, around,

and beneath me, and to recognize God's hand in every element by which I am surrounded. I am grateful, most grateful for this personal benefit.

The next logical direction for Maury's work was to make it international in scope, to include the ships of other nations in his researches. Yet the mere thought of such a scheme in the 1850s was an impossible one. Fierce national jealousies and poor communication between countries had most foreign states eyeing one another with mutual distrust.

Then in the fall of 1851, England asked Daniel Webster, the United States Secretary of State, about the possibility of their two countries co-operating in land-weather observations. Webster passed on the proposal to the Secretary of the Navy's office, where it eventually found its way to Maury. This was just the opening he needed.

In a detailed report Maury explained how the sea covered three-quarters of the earth, thus influencing the weather over land areas. He then suggested an amendment to the British proposition: the establishment of "a universal system of meteorological observations for the sea as well as for the land." To carry out such a plan he added that an international conference might be held, with England, France, Russia, and other countries invited to attend.

It was a bold proposal, but one that caught Daniel Webster's fancy. He enclosed Maury's report along with the official reply to England. Soon Maury found himself authorized to make arrangements for a conference with officials of the various countries. His first contacts were with foreign ministers in Washington, many of whom were his friends or acquaintances. Then he wrote to his scientific correspondents abroad, enlisting their aid. Finally American men of science were invited to assist in formulating a plan for making weather observations on land and sea around the world.

Maury made it clear to Bache and Henry that he himself wanted nothing to do with land-weather observations — that was up to them. All he asked for was their co-operation. His words fell on deaf ears. Neither Bache nor Henry could agree to a government conference rather than one handled by a scientific body. Nor would they ever co-operate in any undertaking organized by Maury. Yet instead of opposing him openly, Henry quietly began writing to influential scientific associates abroad. Soon England and a few of the others had changed their minds and were proposing that land observations should not be included in the conference.

In the end the United States government issued invitations for a conference to adopt a universal system of marine weather observations to be held in Brussels, Belgium, beginning August 23, 1853. Thus the famous Brussels Conference came into being, to be called by some in later years "the first League of Nations."

Maury wanted Nan to go to Brussels with him, but she was never a good traveler, being often in poor health. Besides, she had her youngest ones to care for, and couldn't bear the thought of leaving them behind. Her eighth child, little Lucy, was only two years old. Matthew Jr., known as "Brave," was four, and the solemn-faced Eliza, called "Glum," was seven. So it was decided that the two older girls, Betty and Nannie Curly, would accompany their father along with two teen-age cousins, Ellen Herndon and Ellen Maury. The amused passengers aboard their ship dubbed the bright and talkative group "the Magpie Club."

At every opportunity Maury had always taken one child or another on the various trips he had to make around the country, believing it broadened their education. Even at home he was their principal teacher, especially for the girls, because the education then available for young ladies appalled him. Instead of Latin and Greek, he taught them chemistry and astronomy at the breakfast table, for as he complained in a letter to a friend:

Schools and education disturb me. If I were only a rich man I would devote all my wealth, time, and energies to reforming education. I would build a model college for boys, and another for girls, and be happy as are the angels in the consciousness of doing good. As a general rule, I regard colleges, as at present conducted, as humbug, and female seminaries as downright cheats . . .

Once in Brussels, Maury was in his glory confering with men as intensely interested in the ocean's winds and currents as he himself. They represented Belgium, Denmark, France, England, the Netherlands, Norway, Portugal, Russia, and Sweden. His meeting with Lieutenant Marin H. Jansen of the Netherlands Royal Navy was especially welcome, for the two had previously corresponded at length.

Maury was asked to serve as president of the conference, but he declined, calling on the Belgian representative instead. He did, however, consent to make the opening address. Simply but clearly he outlined the aims of the conference in the elementary French he had learned back in Somerset, Ohio, after his stagecoach accident.

The historic meeting continued for two weeks while the delegates conferred on the number of observations, how and when to make them, and what instruments to use. They were greatly appreciative of Maury's offer in behalf of the United States, to give free charts to ships of any nation agreeing to keep abstract logs. The final decision was a unanimous one in favor of adopting aboard ships of all nations a system of observations similar to the United States Navy's.

Maury and his girls then toured Holland, Germany, and France before returning to the Observatory at the end of October. There he began receiving requests from other nations unable to send representatives to Brussels but desiring to participate in the observations. Maury was delighted. The whole

Brussels venture was turning out to be the highlight of his life. In Berlin the great geographer Alexander von Humboldt had personally congratulated Maury on the results of the conference. Maury was delighted to find that:

> Baron Humboldt is of opinion that the results already obtained from this system of research are sufficient to give rise to a new department of science, which he has called the PHYSICAL GEOGRAPHY OF THE SEA.
>   . . . .
> Rarely before has there been such a sublime spectacle presented to the scientific world: all nations agreeing to unite and co-operate in carrying out one system of philosophical research with regard to the sea. Though they may be enemies in all else, here they are to be friends. Every ship that navigates the high seas with these charts and blank abstract logs on board may henceforth be regarded as a floating observatory, a temple of science.

The physical geography of the sea — a new department of science. It was true. Maury's researches had opened an entirely new field of study. Even the layman was ceasing to regard the ocean as a "waste of waters."

With this thought in mind, Maury's Philadelphia publishers, E. C. & J. Biddle, began urging him to incorporate his findings in a book for the general public. If he did not do it soon, they warned, someone else would. By 1853 Maury's revised *Sailing Directions* (published by Biddle for the Navy Department) was running 772 pages. Despite its title, the book contained a fascinating combination of personal findings, theories, and soaring descriptions of winds and waters. This same information should be copyrighted and offered to the general public, was Biddle's advice. They suggested the larger firm of Harper and Brothers in New York to handle the work, and the more appealing title "The Physical Geography of the Sea."

Maury agreed, and set to work at once drafting a manuscript. Because this was a personal venture, it had to be completed during off-duty hours in the evening. Maury enlisted his entire family's help, as was his custom whenever he was composing speeches or papers. Betty and Nannie Curly were the copyists, either taking dictation or rewriting their father's rough draft. The others were invited to add their comments or criticisms, while little Lucy balanced herself on the arm of his chair and curled his back hair around the red and blue pencil he always used.

The Physical Geography of the Sea was completed in the summer of 1854 and came out early in 1855. It was indeed the great success that Biddle had predicted. During its first year alone five printings were issued, so great was the public response. All together, eight editions in the United States and nineteen in England were published between 1855 and 1861, and the book itself was kept in print by Harper's until 1876. It was reissued by the Harvard University Press in 1963.

It is safe to say that this book was one of the most popular semiscientific works published during the nineteenth century. The opening paragraph of its second chapter, "The Gulf Stream," is perhaps the most widely quoted of Maury's writings, and its style reveals why Maury at once captivated the common man:

> There is a river in the ocean: in the severest droughts it never fails, and in the mightiest floods it never overflows; its banks and its bottom are of cold water, while its current is of warm; the Gulf of Mexico is its fountain, and its mouth is in the Arctic Seas. It is the Gulf Stream . . .

But his enemies were not captivated. The scientists among them objected to his grandiloquent style, to theories unsupported by facts, and to the many Biblical quotations he used. It is true that neither Maury's researches nor his writings ever conformed to the strict scientific methods so dear to university-trained men. Maury called himself a "natural philosopher" rather than a scientist, and it was his purpose to spread new information as quickly and widely as possible. But more than this, his book would stand as a pioneering effort in a department he himself had created: oceanography. Although later researches would prove a few of his theories incorrect, still the interest he had stirred gave momentum to oceanic investigations from that day to the present.

The year 1855 could almost be called the high point of Maury's career. His book was a great success. His Wind and Current Charts were in use around the world. He had received medals and honors from Denmark, Portugal, Belgium, Russia, France, Prussia, the Netherlands, Austria, Sardinia, Sweden, and Norway for his work at the Brussels Conference. He was preparing a new publication on astronomy. Other projects included deep-sea soundings, steamer lanes in the Atlantic, the Atlantic cable, and meteorology for farmers.

It is no wonder, then, that he read his letter of September 17, 1855, from the Secretary of the Navy in stunned disbelief:

> The Board of Naval Officers assembled under the Act to promote the efficiency of the Navy, approved Feb. 28, 1855, having reported you as one of the officers who in their judgment should be placed on the Retired List on leave-of-absence pay, and the findings of the Board having been approved by the President, it becomes my duty to inform you that from this date you are removed from the Active Service List and placed on the Retired List on leave-of-absence pay.
>
> You are, however, not detached from the Naval Observatory. I avail myself the authority of the law to direct that you continue on your present duty.
>
> I am, respectfully, your obedient servant,
> J. C. Dobbin

10 ·
Dark Days

H E WOULD never get over it. Maury, the great promoter of naval reforms, had been cut down by a bill he himself had supported! It had been the purpose of the Naval Retiring Board to make the navy more efficient by determining which of the 700 officers were incapable of performing their duties properly. The Board met secretly and eliminated 201 officers, most of them older men and ready for retirement. But Maury was only forty-nine and at the peak of his career.

At long last his enemies were having their revenge. The jealous ones who resented his fame at home and abroad . . . the disgruntled ones who felt he should serve his time at sea like the rest of them . . . the bitter ones whom he had criticized in his "Lucky Bag" articles . . . perhaps even his civilian enemies who had friends on the Board.

The Board itself remained silent after its action. It would neither explain its decisions nor reverse them. But it was hinted that the excuse used for Maury's retirement was his crippled leg.

"There were members of that Board, I am told, who behaved like hungry wolves and shocked others by the display of savage enmity," declared Maury. "It's a wicked Board to distract my attention from useful work and concentrate it on these miserable controversies," he added in typical Maury fashion.

But if Maury had enemies, he also had friends just as loud in their praise of him and as fierce in their condemnation of the Board. Retire Maury? Why, he should be promoted! The United States Navy should be ashamed of itself for keeping a man of Maury's position a mere lieutenant for all these years!

One of the Navy secretaries he had served under wrote him:

> . . . on no duty either ashore or afloat could your services have been as valuable to the country or as distinguishing and honourable to your profession, as that to which you have been so assigned.

The hue and cry raised over the Retiring Board's

action finally caused Congress to pass another bill a year later granting all officers who had been retired the right to request a naval court of inquiry. Maury's case did not come up for still another year, in November 1857, at which time he conducted his own defense. Finally in January 1858, Maury was not only restored to active duty but also promoted to the rank of commander, to be effective from September 14, 1855, the date of his "retirement."

During his two-and-a-half years of efforts to reverse the Board's ruling, Maury was kept on duty at the Observatory and expected to perform his regular tasks. This he did with his typical navy loyalty, for it was the Board that had discredited him, he believed, not the navy. But his family was hard pressed to live on the $1,200 leave-of-absence pay. Even his regular salary of $3,000 had been meager enough in view of the entertaining he had to do. Friends, relatives, fellow officers, and foreign dignitaries had made it a habit to drop in on the genial Lieutenant Maury whenever they were in Washington. He welcomed all to his home and to his table with true Southern hospitality, even though Nan often wondered where the next meal was coming from.

Maury worked as hard as ever during these years of "retirement." But he was handicapped by not having as full support for his projects as he had had in earlier years before he became a controversial figure. His professional rivals even became so bold as to steal one of his research vessels out from under his nose!

The issue at stake was the laying of a telegraphic underwater cable across the Atlantic Ocean between Newfoundland and Ireland. Cyrus Field, its promoter, had asked Maury in 1853 if such an undertaking were possible. Maury was pleased to inform him that Lieutenant Berryman of his staff had just completed deep-sea soundings across the North Atlantic which revealed the presence of an underwater plateau all the way across. Moreover, samples taken from the bottom were composed entirely of microscopic shells in perfect condition. "Indeed," Maury wrote, "these soundings suggest the idea that the sea, like the snow-cloud with its flakes in a calm, is always letting fall upon its bed showers of these microscopic shells." Maury interpreted this unique finding to mean that the bottom was perfectly calm with no currents to harm an underwater cable.

Maury's so-called "telegraphic plateau" seemed made to order for an Atlantic cable. But his scientific enemies in Washington remained unconvinced. Because Maury was not a university-trained scientist like themselves, they would never believe that any of his findings were truly reliable. They continued to refer to him as a "pretender" and a "charlatan." They succeeded in casting enough doubt on his report to make more soundings necessary. Maury requested three vessels for this purpose from the Secretary of the Navy in May 1856, but he was refused on the grounds that there were none available.

Little did he know that Professor Bache already had the Secretary's ear through a mutual friend, Jefferson Davis, the Secretary of War. Davis was also a Regent of the Smithsonian and a great admirer of Bache and Henry. At every opportunity he pressed for support of the Smithsonian Institution's projects and those of the United States Coast Survey in place of the Naval Observatory's.

Now in June of 1856, as Maury left Washington for a speaking engagement, Bache quickly put into action a plan he and his friends had devised to put the deep-sea sounding project under the Coast Survey's control. He requested the naval vessel *Arctic* to be sent out immediately to survey the North Atlantic. No questions were asked, for most of the Coast Survey's work was carried out by naval vessels and personnel lent to them for the purpose. The fact that Bache was restricted to work within sixty miles of the coast was no barrier this time, for he was still smarting under Maury's invasion of his territory the year before when Maury had carried out navy orders to rechart the approaches to New York harbor.

Maury was furious when he returned home and discovered what was happening. He went straight to the Secretary of the Navy, demanding that all information collected be sent directly to the Observatory. This was eventually carried out, but the results were disconcerting. The soundings recorded in the vessel's log did not agree with those plotted on its chart. Nor did the soundings made on the outbound trip agree with those made in the same areas on the return voyage. Moreover, none of the data agreed with Maury's orginal findings. Maury blamed it on the faulty techniques and instruments used, but there was also the possibility that they had been purposely changed to confuse him.

The whole affair was an unfortunate one. Maury would never understand why rivalries like this should be allowed to block scientific progress. But he would always fight for the Observatory when he felt its honor was at stake.

Cyrus Field would not take either side. Yet he appreciated Maury's unfailing support during the many discouraging years before the first successful Atlantic cable was laid. At a banquet in New York in 1858 celebrating the first message sent across the Atlantic, Field declared: "I am a man of few words: Maury furnished the brains, England gave the money, and I did the work."

But the project that meant most to Maury during these years was his land-weather observation scheme, which he called "meteorology for the farmers." It was his belief that farmers could record and report the weather on land just as mariners were doing at sea. The results would then be assembled at the Observatory and telegraphed across the country as daily weather reports.

This time his chief rival was Professor Henry at the Smithsonian. Maury knew of Henry's work in the weather field, and had even tried to enlist his aid in the farmer project at first. When Henry showed little interest in the scheme, Maury decided to attempt it on his own. It was as grand a plan as his abstract ships' logs, and could eventually result in just as beneficial a service to farmers as the Wind and Current Charts had been to mariners, he believed.

But Henry was appalled at the thought of common farmers being called upon to perform a scientific chore. He would use every power at his command to block the plan. At first Maury couldn't believe that Henry really considered him a rival. Even when newspaper articles hinted as much, Maury was not convinced. He explained in a letter to one of his cousins:

> Three or four weeks ago an article came out in the *Tribune,* saying my plan was intended to act as a rival to that of the Smithsonian. I knew the notion would be injurious to the working of the meteorological plan if it got out, so I wrote a letter to the *Tribune* in my own name to show what Henry of the Smithsonian was after, and what I was after, and that the two plans were no more rivals of each other than the astronomical observatories which are springing up in various parts of the country are to this one. So far from being rivals, they are quite the contrary . . .

At the January 1856 meeting of the United States Agricultural Society in Washington, Henry's true feelings became evident. After Maury's speech to the group in which he set forth his plan, Henry spoke at length about the Smithsonian's weather work. He then pointed out that though Maury's work in charting winds and currents at sea was important, it was a simple matter involving no particular scientific ability — nothing, for instance, that would prepare a man for devising a land-weather plan. Henry denied any rivalry between himself and Maury, saying that he only represented the Institution, whereas Maury seemed to do everything in his own name, although at the expense of the government. Maury was shocked that a scientific man would permit himself to voice such expressions of petty jealousy.

Many members of the Society, however, were inclined to favor Maury, the practical scientist who believed that plain men like themselves could assist in scientific research. Yet in the end, Henry's supporters carried the day by defeating a Meteorology for the Farmers Bill in Congress.

After this Maury carried his appeal directly to the people on a lecture tour of twelve cities in 1858 and again in 1859. By then it was too late, for already the storm clouds of the coming Civil War had arisen across the nation.

Maury's attitude toward slavery was similar to that of many enlightened Southern gentlemen. He believed it to be a curse and a blot upon his fair Virginia, but he could see no immediate end to it. Whereas his friends and relatives in the North condemned slavery as immoral, Maury looked to the Bible as was his custom and found nothing there forbidding the practice.

As Maury declared to one of his relatives:

> I am sure you would rejoice to see the people of Virginia rise up to-morrow and say . . . there shall be neither slavery nor involuntary servitude in Virginia. Although this would not strike the shackle from off a single arm, nor command a single slave to go free, yet it would relieve our own loved Virginia of that curse. Such an act on the part of the State would cause slave-owners generally either to leave the State with their slaves, or to send them off to the Southern markets.

A far more important issue, it seemed to Maury, was the stiff protective tariff which favored the industrial North at the expense of the agricultural South. Yet surely a satisfactory solution to all of the trouble could be found. Maury never once allowed himself to be pessimistic about this or any other issue. Of course, the problem could be solved by men of good will!

By 1860 there were few men of good will to be found in either North or South. Tempers and opinions had risen to a fever pitch. "Abolish slavery!" rang like a battle cry from Northern pulpits and town squares. "Secede from the Union!" was the answering echo from state after state in the South.

Maury was on a trip to England to secure a copyright for a new edition of his *Physical Geography*

when Abraham Lincoln won the November election. Maury had supported John Bell, a Southern conservative who upheld both the Union and slavery, but he had come in a poor third in the electoral votes. By the time Maury returned to Washington in December, South Carolina had already seceded.

At once he began a letter-writing campaign, aimed first at the governor of New Jersey to persuade his state to mediate between the North and the South. He chose New Jersey because it was the only one of the original states that had never passed any legislation unfriendly toward the South. When nothing came of this plan, Maury approached Pennsylvania and then Maryland and Delaware with the same proposition.

Now events were rapidly drawing to a climax with state after Southern state seceding, and Maury wrote with greater urgency to influential friends. The Union must not be allowed to dissolve! Virginia must stay in! The issue was not cotton nor slavery nor Lincoln's election, he emphasized, but that fact that the South was completely blocked by a Northern majority in Congress. Give the South a vote in the Senate to establish a balance of power, and the Union might be saved.

He called on former President John Tyler. He wrote to friends in England. He pleaded with powerful men in the South not to secede, or if their state was already out, then not to start a war. For if war came, there was only one honorable course for a man like Maury. He could not bear arms against his homeland and his kin. And he could not remain an officer in the United States Navy unless he were willing to fight. As he wrote to a friend:

> The line of duty, therefore, is to me clear — each one to follow his own State, if his own State goes to war; if not, he may remain to help on the work of reunion.
>
> If there be no war between the sections, we must hoist the flag of re-annexation, to carry the elections of '64 upon that issue, bring back the seceding States, and be happier and greater, and more glorious than ever.

On April 12 South Carolina bombarded the Union Fort Sumter in Charleston Harbor. On April 15 President Lincoln called for 75,000 volunteer troops. On April 17 Virginia voted to secede from the Union rather than be forced to fight against her sister states. On April 20, 1861, Matthew Fontaine Maury wrote one of the shortest and most painful letters of his life:

> His Excellency, Abraham Lincoln, President of the United States,
>
> I beg leave herewith to resign into your hands my commission as a Commander in the Navy of the United States.
>
> > Respectfully,
> > M. F. Maury

11 ·
War

So WAR had come. And nothing that Matthew Maury or the governors of the states or even the President himself could do would have stopped it. It was as if a great dam had suddenly burst across the nation, releasing a tide of emotions pent up for years. There was no possible turning back — nor any desire to. The North went off to fight a great "holy" war to preserve the Union and to abolish slavery. For the South it would be a war of independence, a fight to preserve a way of life.

"All of us are of one mind —" wrote Maury to his former teacher and life-long friend, William Hasbrouck from Newburgh, New York, "very cool, very determined; no desire for a conflict. We are on the defensive. We have nothing to fight the North about; but if the North wants a fight, it can have it. We are ready; but the North must come to us for it . . ."

Of the 1,400 naval officers in the United States in 1861, 230 had, like Maury, joined the Confederacy. But Maury was by far the most notorious. Northern newspapers that had been singing his praises for years were stung to the quick by his defection. Soon a vicious campaign against America's great "Pathfinder of the Seas" spread through the Northern press. His professional enemies hurried to join the fray, discrediting his name wherever they could. Wild stories about the damage and sabotage he had done to lighthouses and buoys before he quit his post ran rampant through the North, causing President Lincoln to refuse his resignation. Almost no other public figure in the South was so condemned. Maury was shocked to read in a Boston paper:

> $5,000 reward for the Head of Jeff Davis
> $3,000 for the Head of Gen. Beauregard
> $3,000 for the Head of the Traitor, Lieut. Maury

But he quickly recovered and wrote to a friend:

> A price has been set on my head in Boston. I thank them for the honour; for I do not forget that in other days a price was set upon the heads of the best men of that State, and the cause in which I fight is far more righteous than that which moved

those great and good men to take up arms against their mother-country.

Immediately upon leaving Washington, Maury reported to Virginia Governor John Letcher in Richmond, and was asked to serve on an Advisory Council of Three to help the state mobilize for invasion. He was glad his family was settled elsewhere, although he missed them sorely. Nan and the younger children were staying with cousins in Fredericksburg. The two older boys, Dick and "Davy Jones" (John), were attending the University of Virginia (but eventually left to join the Confederate army). The two older girls, now married, were with their husbands in Fredericksburg.

The most important single service the Advisory Council performed was its decision to raise the hull of the U.S.S. *Merrimac,* burned and sunk by Federal forces before they evacuated the Norfolk Navy Yard. It would eventually be converted into one of the world's first ironclad warships, the C.S.S. *Virginia.*

Next Maury concentrated on defending Virginia's vulnerable waterways. The Potomac River, the Rappahannock, the York, and the James all offered the enemy wide avenues for invasion. Richmond itself could easily be captured by a Federal fleet steaming up the James. The state might boast a strong and dedicated corps of naval officers and men, but it had no ships of war. The grounded navy was therefore put in charge of batteries being built along every river and bay.

To far-sighted Maury, this was not enough. He knew firsthand every detail of the Federal navy's overpowering strength and every weakness in Virginia's sad state of defense. No, the South must look to other means besides conventional weapons, if she would survive and win her independence. Almost at once Maury turned his attention to an ingenious but terrible device: the "torpedo," a fixed mine planted underwater and exploded either mechanically or electrically.

Both Robert Fulton and Samuel Colt had experimented with torpedoes, but no one had successfully set them off electrically in actual warfare. It was Maury's belief that all of Virginia's wide network of waterways could be best defended by electric torpedoes. Governor Letcher had great faith in Maury's judgment and enough daring to back such a novel scheme. At once an agent was secretly dispatched to the North to procure the necessary insulated wire which was totally lacking in the South. But the man failed, and Maury was finally forced to find a mechanical means for exploding his underwater charges.

Meanwhile, the Confederate government moved its capital from Montgomery, Alabama, to Richmond. Virginia's forces were of course turned over to the Confederacy, but not without friction over new rules and procedures. Throughout the war the Confederacy would be plagued by this conflict between its sovereign states and central government.

To Maury it became a serious difficulty indeed,

for the Confederate government was headed by his sworn enemies. Its President, Jefferson Davis, had conspired with Bache against him. Its Secretary of the Navy, Stephen Mallory, had led the fight in the Senate against restoring Maury to active duty during the Retiring Board controversy. Several other senior Confederate naval officers had been members of the notorious Board. Maury's sacrifice for his native state was truly a total one. His career as a great naval hydrographer was finished; his usefulness to the South was in the hands of enemies.

For the moment, though, he continued his work on torpedoes undisturbed. In the bedroom of a cousin's house in Richmond he began his search for a foolproof method of exploding his weapons. He experimented with tiny submerged powder charges in a washtub, trying every means possible to set them off. At last in July he seemed to have solved the problem. With makeshift equipment put together by himself and the Tredegar Iron Works of Richmond, he was ready for the first trial.

Down to Norfolk he secretly made his way at night, to Sewell's Point across the harbor from the great Federal bastion, Fortress Monroe. There, silhouetted in the moonlight, were the distant outlines of five Federal vessels at anchor. Maury knew he must have more information before proceeding with his attack, so he sent out some of his helpers to scout enemy activity. It was an hour's row across Hampton Roads harbor, but at last they returned with the re-

port of a small steamer which patrolled the area periodically.

Finally on July 7 Maury launched his attack. Each of five rowboats held a double torpedo rig consisting of two kegs filled with two hundred pounds of powder and triggered by a long span connecting each. The kegs were weighted to sink to twenty feet, while the cork span would float on the surface, drift against the hull of a ship, set off two fuses, and explode the kegs. Maury rode in the lead boat with a pilot and four oarsmen. They had waited till the moon set, but the tide was with them, for they would need its action to carry the torpedoes to their targets.

Now as they approached the two largest ships, all was silent. Maury whispered the order to release the torpedoes. With their spans bobbing along the surface, they drifted underwater toward the unsuspecting targets. There was no sign of the patrol steamer.

Quickly Maury ordered the boats away: all were

130

to return to Norfolk but his own. He would stand off a short distance to witness the results. As the spans stretched tight against the ships' hulls they should trigger the torpedo fuses, which would burn for fifty-four seconds before exploding the powder.

Maury peered through the darkness, but the spans were no longer visible. Had they reached the ships? The waiting became unbearable. Surely they were at the ships by now! Why didn't they go off? What was wrong? An hour passed. No use waiting any longer. The crestfallen inventor finally returned to shore to begin again. Later he would discover that his fuses would not burn any deeper than fifteen feet underwater. Five feet of water had stood between success and failure that night. It was the first known use of torpedoes in warfare.

The following day the crew of the U.S.S. *Resolute* picked up a pair of objects that had drifted north with the tide up as far as the Potomac River. Had they only known who sent them on their way, what an outcry there would have been in the North! For in those days of gentlemanly warfare, such sinister weapons as torpedoes were considered immoral. Even Nan opposed Maury's work in this field, and Maury himself had his doubts until Lincoln set the tone of the war by declaring all medicines and surgical instruments to be contraband. Still Maury had to admit: "This business of blowing up men while they are asleep, I don't glory in, I shall endeavor to pick up and save the crews from drowning."

When the fuse problem was at last solved, Maury approached Secretary Mallory for funds for the wide-scale development of torpedoes. Mallory promptly refused, believing it only another of what he considered to be Maury's harebrained schemes. But Governor Letcher's support remained as firm as ever, and he assigned Maury two barrels of blasting powder to be used in a demonstration to convince Mallory of the torpedo's worth.

The demonstration was held in the James River just below Richmond. Maury and his son Dick rowed a huge oaken beer keg filled with powder out to mid-channel and lowered it to the bottom. Then they rowed clear, trailing a lanyard attached to the trigger. At a given signal Maury pulled the lanyard and there was an instantaneous explosion with a geyser of mud and water erupting twenty feet in the air. Mallory was convinced, and the Confederate Congress eventually appropriated $50,000 for torpedo warfare.

But Maury could not rest at that. He was convinced that this was the perfect time and place for his old idea of big guns and small ships. A fleet of swift little Confederate gunboats could wreak havoc among the Federal frigates now blockading Southern ports. Taking up his pen again, he began a series of letters to the editor of the Richmond *Enquirer* urging this plan and several others. He signed his letters "Ben Bow," but this time fooled no one. His style, his ideas, and his methods were too well known in Richmond.

The results he got were swift but wholly unexpected. Two days after his first letter appeared, he was taken off torpedo work and put on special assignment to purchase arms in Cuba. Maury was dumfounded. Any junior officer could have carried out the arms mission, while only he knew the intricacies of the torpedo work. It was obvious he was being got rid of by his enemies. He was even more sure when he learned he was to run the Federal blockade from New Orleans in a sailboat. Even a fast Confederate steamer had been unable to get out for two months.

All of Richmond was outraged when they learned of Maury's "banishment." His influential Virginia friends would have none of it. They raised such a fuss that the Cuba order was finally canceled, Maury was put back on torpedo work, and even his gunboat plan was adopted. It was never carried to completion, for in the meantime the ironclad *Merrimac* (rechristened *Virginia*) made her appearance, spelling doom to the future of all wooden ships.

Then in the spring of 1862, incredible as it seems, ten miles of insulated wire were washed ashore at Norfolk from an underwater telegraph line at Fortress Monroe. Now Maury had the final ingredient for his electric torpedoes. By mid-June he had successfully mined the James River with them, and

134

could turn over the work to the assistant he had trained, Lieutenant Hunter Davidson of the mine layer C.S.S. *Teaser*.

Davidson had the misfortune to lose his ship less than a month later in the river when a shell from a Union vessel exploded her boiler. Worst of all — or so it seemed at first — many of Maury's torpedo plans fell into enemy hands. The United States immediately carried out torpedo experiments near Baltimore following Maury's directions. Their effectiveness was vividly demonstrated when one ship was blown to pieces. Thereafter, the James River and most other waterways suspected of being mined were safe from Union penetration. All together, forty Federal ships were sunk by torpedoes during the war, and to United States sailors they were one of the most dreaded weapons of the South.

Now that Maury's experimental phase of the torpedo work was finished, he turned to other tasks. More than anything else, he wanted to command a fighting ship. For once Mallory was sympathetic and offered him the only thing then available, the command of a tiny gunboat in Charleston harbor. Maury mulled it over, but when he found that the vessel was too small to go to sea, he decided it was not for him.

Finally, in August, his superiors had an assignment for him: he was to go to England on secret service to purchase torpedo materials and vessels for the South. He was well known there, with many influential friends. Perhaps he could even help gain England's recognition of the Confederacy. Maury had no choice but to accept such an important mission — or was it another attempt to get rid of him?

I 2 ·

To England

MAURY decided to take his thirteen-year-old-son "Brave" (Matthew, Jr.) along and put him in school in England. A third member of the party was Midshipman James M. Morgan, assigned as Maury's aide and later to be a junior officer aboard the Confederate warship Maury was to purchase.

They made their first attempt to run the Union blockade from Charleston, South Carolina, on the night of September 24, 1862, in the steamer *Hero,* but Federal warships off the Charleston bar turned them back. The *Hero* repeated its efforts to slip away every dark night thereafter, but with no success. On

October 9 it seemed cloudy enough to try again, this time in a different ship since the *Hero* was too well known. They boarded the much smaller coastal steamer *Herald* and were approaching the bar when suddenly the clouds parted to reveal a Union sloop-of-war dead ahead in the moonlight. Quickly the little steamer reversed course and retreated to port under heavy fire.

Impatient to be off on his mission, Maury spent his days discussing affairs with Confederate officers in Charleston or writing to his family. If he ever got away, he would let them know by a carrier pigeon to be released at sea. Its Charleston owner would then forward the news to Nan.

Finally, on the drizzly night of October 12, the little *Herald* steamed out of the harbor, nearly grounded herself on the bar, but scraped across unchallenged into the open sea. They were off for British Bermuda, the first leg of the voyage to England.

Once at sea, it was soon evident that the *Herald* was never built to battle the raging main. Towering waves and gale-force winds tossed her about like a matchstick. Maury, Brave, and most of the passengers took to their bunks miserably seasick. Meanwhile, the vessel shipped so much water that her engine broke down. They wallowed about helplessly until it could be repaired, expecting any moment to be seized by patrolling Federal warships.

By this time they had drifted so far off course that

in addition to their troubles, they were hopelessly lost. The captain was a coastal navigator, unfamiliar with the open sea but too proud to admit his ignorance to a naval officer like Maury. Finally on the sixth day he confided to Maury that something terrible must have happened, for they had just sailed over the spot where the Bermuda Islands were supposed to be.

Maury told the man he would have to slow down his vessel and wait, for there was nothing that could be done until the moon came out at ten o'clock that night. At ten P.M. Maury appeared on deck with a sextant in one hand and a notebook in the other. He proceeded to take his observations and make his calculations slowly and carefully, completely unperturbed. At times he lay flat on his back, squinting through the sextant at the moon or the tiny pinpoints of light in the night sky he knew so well. The entire host of passengers was his breathless audience. But when he took longer and longer, they grew impatient. Finally, with great calmness and complete assurance Maury told the captain the course to steer and the speed, informing him that he would sight the light at Port Hamilton, Bermuda, at two A.M. Then the great hydrographer and his son retired for the night.

No one else could think of turning in. All peered ahead through the darknes, anxiously awaiting the given hour. When two o'clock arrived the sea was still as dark and empty as before. At five past two there was still no sight of a light. People began to grumble that they knew there was too much science aboard. The minutes slipped by, and then at ten past two the masthead lookout cried, "Light ho!" and Maury's reputation was once again secure.

Their four-day stay in Bermuda was one of great satisfaction for Maury after the difficult years he had just gone through. For here he was still "the great Lieutenant Maury," a renowned and respected scientist. Midshipman Morgan was amazed at his chief's reception here and in Europe. Like most Americans, he had no idea Maury was so well known or highly esteemed abroad. It had been Europe that had offered Maury refuge when America's Civil War broke out. Both the Grand Duke Constantine of Russia and Napoleon III of France had invited Maury to live in their countries and pursue his studies in peace. He was greatly tempted, but his commitment to Virginia came first.

Now in Bermuda he was royally entertained at the Government House, as well as being honored with a dinner aboard a British man-of-war in the harbor. Later when they departed for Halifax, Nova Scotia, aboard a British Royal Mail steamer, the same man-of-war cruised near by, preventing two United States sloops-of-war from causing trouble.

In Halifax, Maury again experienced a warm reception. A Confederate flag was flown from the hotel in his honor, and all day long hand organs in the street below played "Dixie."

At last in mid-November Maury boarded the great Cunard paddle-wheel steamer *Arabia* for the final voyage to Liverpool. Once there, he reported to Captain James D. Bulloch, Confederate secret agent in England, and then commenced his mission.

Midshipman Morgan was again overwhelmed by the string of fancy carriages lined up in front of Maury's London quarters as England's leaders came to pay their respects to America's great "Pathfinder of the Seas." Even Marin Jansen from Holland came across the Channel to visit his old friend.

Since Maury was engaged in secret work, many details are lacking concerning his days in England. It is known that he continued work with torpedoes, sending back both information and equipment for their improvement. He also attempted to interest the British in the Confederate cause, but soon realized that sympathy for the South was more imagined than real. He worked closely with a group called the "Society for Obtaining the Cessation of Hostilities," which was circulating a petition calling for the halt of the Civil War and for Southern independence. But perhaps his most important accomplishment was the purchase of a vessel to be used as one of the famed Confederate commerce raiders against the Union.

Maury bought the uncompleted 550-ton iron screw steamer in Scotland. His cousin Lieutenant Lewis Maury, who would be its commander, secretly joined him and set about outfitting the vessel. The ship was launched in March 1863 under the name of the *Japan,* and an English crew was signed on for a two-year voyage to Singapore. No armaments could be installed until she was in international waters or the British would have impounded her.

The presence in England of secret agents working for the Union brought added danger. These agents immediately put the *Japan* under surveillance, knowing the Confederates would have to slip her out and arm her at sea. They suspected that a smaller arms boat would rendezvous with the *Japan* off the island of Alderney. Here they planned to intercept her. Fortunately Maury's people learned their plans, and the arms boat with Lewis and Midshipman Morgan aboard was redirected to meet the *Japan* off the French port of Ushant.

Once on board Lewis renamed the vessel C.S.S. *Georgia,* and commissioned her as a warship in the Confederate States Navy. When her crew discovered her true purpose, some asked to be returned to England, which was done. But many were happy to serve on a commerce raider, for they would be earning a share of every prize she captured.

The Union loathed these "pirates," as it called them, which preyed on defenseless merchant vessels, forgetting it too had used the same tactics against the British in the War of 1812. Although the *Georgia* lasted only seven months before she broke down, her career as a commerce raider was a remarkable one.

Assigned to the South Atlantic, she captured her

first prize, the *Dictator* with a cargo of coal, on April 25 off the Cape Verde Islands. After the crew were taken on board as prisoners, the ship was burned. On June 8 the clipper ship *George Griswold* with a cargo of coal was captured off Rio de Janiero. She was allowed to go free after posting a bond, and all prisoners were transferred to her. Four days later the bark *Good Hope* was taken, her cargo and crew removed, and the ship burned. On June 14 the bark *J. W. Seaver,* bound for Russia with machinery, was captured and bonded. On June 25 the ship *Constitution,* bound for Shanghai with coal, was captured. Then followed the capture of the *City of Bath* off Brazil, the *Prince of Wales* and the *John Watts* in mid-south Atlantic, and the *Bold Hunter* off French West Africa.

When the *Georgia* finally anchored at Cherbourg, France, in October, she had destroyed untold tons of Union shipping and bonded many more for over $200,000.

Maury succeeded in buying one other vessel in England, but it was forced to flee to Calais, France, where it was bottled up in the harbor by two Union vessels for the remainder of the war.

Despite the respect and attention given him by influential Englishmen, Maury's stay in England was not an especially pleasant one. He disliked undercover work, his health was poor, and he desperately missed his family. Nightmares about their sufferings haunted his dreams. In the spring of 1863 he was horrified to learn that some of these dreams were true: his son Davy was missing in action along the Mississippi and was never again found. Shortly afterwards he learned that Dick had been shot through the hips and might be crippled for life.

But Maury never gave in or gave up. He forced himself to keep busy during his final year in England, spending most of his time on torpedo work, until two kidney operations slowed him down. He was no longer a young man, having passed his fifty-eighth birthday in January 1864.

Spring brought the depressing news of General Lee's surrender at Appomattox Court House, but not necessarily the end of the war so far as many Southerners were concerned. Maury decided to return home with the $40,000 worth of torpedo equipment he had assembled for one last desperate stand in the ports of Texas. He and Brave boarded the Royal Mail Steamer for St. Thomas in the West Indies, and set out May 2 on a voyage that would finally take Maury even further from his beloved home.

13.
New Virginia, Mexico

WHEN he arrived in St. Thomas, Maury learned of the Confederacy's almost total collapse. Continuing on to Cuba, he found the news there even more discouraging. To go on to the Texas ports seemed useless. Besides, he was warned by friends not to think of returning to the United States where only imprisonment awaited him. At once Maury decided to put his emergency plan into operation. He would lay down his own arms by writing a letter of surrender and putting his torpedo material ashore. Then he would arrange for Brave to return to Virginia, while he himself set out for Mexico.

145

His plan was a bold but desperate one: to transplant the Southern plantation culture bodily from Virginia to Mexico. He would approach Maximilian, ruler of the new French Empire in Mexico (whom he already knew through scientific correspondence), and ask him to open Mexico to colonization by the defeated Southern planters. It would be the perfect land of refuge, where Southerners whose plantations had been ravaged could start again and rebuild anew their cherished way of life. Furthermore, it would

give Maximilian, whose rule was never too secure, a strong and loyal group of supporters to develop the country and make it great.

Maury landed at Vera Cruz, crossed the hot lowlands, and began his ascent to the high plateaus of the interior by rail and stagecoach. He was greatly impressed by the grandeur of the scenery and the luxuriance of nature. "What do you think of coffee growing wild, of fig-trees 100 feet high and three feet in circumference, and the most luscious pine-apples at a cent apiece?" he wrote home to his family.

He halted at Cordoba in a fertile mountain valley 55 miles from Vera Cruz and 2,700 feet above sea level. Its climate seemed ideal, and near by stood the remains of the great abandoned haciendas of the conquistadores. "In the olden times, Cordova was the garden spot of New Spain," wrote Maury. "There stands on one side, and but a little way off, the Peak of Orizaba, with its cap of everlasting snow, and on the other the sea in full view."

This would be the site of his "New Virginia" if the Emperor agreed. "If he is wise and will encourage my plans I can assist mightily to make firm the foundations of his dynasty . . . If I can pave the way for the introduction into that country of enough good Southern blood to leaven the whole lump, then I think I shall be doing a greater service . . . than I could by making forecasts of the weather . . . "

Again Maury's main concern was to perform a useful service. But this time his imagination had carried him too far afield. Almost none of his Virginia friends agreed with his colonization scheme. His family and relatives were wholly opposed, with the exception of Dick, who felt too bitter about defeat to live in the States. Some urged Maury to return to England and wait awhile until the North's vengeance against Confederate leaders had run its course. Many could not believe he would actually desert his native state altogether. All were worried about the possible physical danger to anyone closely connected with the puppet ruler, Maximilian. Even Marin Jansen wrote from Holland: "I never met a man of such high intellect who was so much led astray by his own imagination as you are." Perhaps the most cutting comment of all was from a New York cousin who wrote: "You are at least twenty years too old for any such undertaking."

Nevertheless, Maury proceeded with his plans. He was not a man who could stand aside and do nothing for his people in their dark hour of defeat when some action was possible. And it was true that many Confederates did look toward Mexico as a possible refuge. Some, in fact, had already crossed the Rio Grande.

Both Maximilian and his wife Carlota looked with favor on the plan, and in September 1865 Maury was appointed Imperial Commissioner of Colonization.

From the beginning his task was a hopeless one. Maximilian was a weak ruler, full of good intentions but without the ability to carry them out. The Mexican ministers in his government resented the fact that Maury was soon a favorite of the Emperor. The Mexican aristocracy strongly opposed any foreigners who might take over their lands or their position in society. The Mexican people as a whole were totally against the French Empire, which had been forced upon them by foreign troops.

Then there was the United States to contend with. Northern papers at once pounced upon Maury's scheme as "slavery in disguise." It was true that planters were urged to bring any loyal "servants," but since slavery had long been outlawed in Mexico, these were to be "apprentices" (indentured servants) for a certain number of years. Dick, however, informed his father that he doubted whether any Negros would emigrate with their former masters. Nor would the United States have permitted them to go.

Meanwhile, Confederates began arriving in Mexico to look for land. Maury established his "Carlotta Colony" near Cordoba, even though the land situation was far from settled. Much surveying had to be done. Clear titles were hard to obtain. Poor transportation and communication added to their difficulties.

Still Maury continued to write glowing reports to Nan in Virginia, hoping to persuade her to join him:

> Two ship-loads of immigrants have just arrived. Sheridan had refused to let them embark at New Orleans, as he was "determined to break up that Maury nest of Confederates which was agitating the public mind of the South, and preventing the people there from quietly submitting to subjugation." I thank him for the encouragement. We are going to have happy times, a fine country, and a bright future here.

Dick and his wife arrived in October, to Maury's great joy. The young man decided to purchase 640 acres in the Carlotta Colony and send to China for laborers. Nan would come also if Maury insisted, but with great misgivings. Since conditions were still far from settled, Maury at last decided to have his family go to England. He would join them for a visit in the spring as soon as his work allowed it.

Meanwhile, Maximilian's ministers seemed to be stalling Maury at every turn. The truth was, they greatly desired recognition of their government by the United States, and knew that a Confederate colony within their borders was sure to cause them trouble in this respect.

In March 1866 Maury was granted leave by the Emperor to visit his family in England, and to buy instruments for a National Observatory in Mexico City which he would head. Except for Brave, he had not seen any of them for three and a half years full of unparalleled trouble and hardship. Now "Tots" (Mary) was already grown at twenty-one, "Glum" (Eliza) at nineteen was still as quiet and serious as ever, and his "baby," Lucy, was almost fourteen.

But when Maury himself walked into their London quarters one night late in March, the family greeted him in stunned disbelief. Lucy broke the silence as she blurted out, "This is not my papa! This is an old man with a white beard!"

14·
Professor

IT WAS true — the war had aged Maury beyond his years. Davy's loss alone had turned his beard white overnight. But having his family close again cheered him as nothing else could. Even Maximilian's letter in April, informing him that the colonization plans had been canceled, did not upset Maury as much as it could have, now that his strength had been renewed in the presence of his loved ones. Perhaps he had suspected as much before he left Mexico. Although he was invited to return to head the National Observatory, Maury declined with thanks. The Mexican venture had not been for personal gain, but to help his defeated people.

Mexico's Confederate colonies immediately dissolved, their occupants scattering to the four winds. Dick and his family went on to Nicaragua for the next few years. Soon all traces of Maury's presence in Mexico had vanished, but for one. He had conceived the idea that the Mexican plateau might be an ideal spot for growing chinchona trees, whose bark was the source of quinine, the important malaria preventive. Therefore he had arranged with the British in India to ship three parcels of the seed to Mexico, where it was duly planted and did indeed thrive.

Now in England, Maury was again without work or money. The Confederate defeat had wiped out his savings in America, and he was anxious to rebuild a college fund for his children. The quickest way seemed to be by selling the unique knowledge he had accumulated about torpedo warfare. He therefore invited interested governments to participate in a course he would give on torpedoes.

France was the first to respond. He was invited to Paris in May to lecture on and demonstrate electric mining. Afterwards he conducted similar courses in England for representatives from Sweden, Holland, and Britain. Soon the facts about his weapon were so generally known that no other country had need of his services.

Then a London testimonial dinner in his honor greatly aided his college fund, for he was presented with a purse of three thousand guineas in appreciation of his long years of service to the maritime nations of the world.

But Maury was as always the man of action who had to be doing something for the benefit of someone somewhere. His next opportunity came from a New York publisher who wanted to know if he would prepare a series of school geographies, to be sold in the States. He would. He approached the task with his customary originality and was soon writing a beginner's book which took students on an imaginary tour around the world. It was a radical departure from the dry treatment of geography in other school texts. Making learning interesting seemed a shocking innovation to some teachers. But his books endured for many generations, and his style was later copied so often as to make it the commonplace approach. Said Maury about his geographies: "I could not wind up my career more usefully — and usefulness is both, honor and glory — than by helping to shape the character and mould the destinies of the rising generations."

Talk of winding up his career was much too premature. His new role as teacher had hardly begun. Ever since the war's end he had been receiving offers from various colleges in the South. Now in 1868 he decided to accept an especially tempting one: that of professor of physics at Virginia's top science school, the Virginia Military Institute at Lexington. His main task would be to help rebuild his state by conducting a physical survey of Virginia.

Whether or not he would be allowed back in the States was a chance he would have to take. His name was still on a list of about three hundred Confederates who had not been granted amnesty. But word had come through that others on the list had returned home unchallenged.

Before Maury left England, one more honor came his way: he was awarded a Doctor of Laws degree from Cambridge University. The Latin presentation address was especially heartwarming, for the English could appreciate his great sacrifice during the war better than those more closely involved in the States. In part the translation of it read:

> When that cruel Civil War in America was imminent, this man did not hestitate to leave home and friends, a place of high honour and an office singularly adapted to his genius — to throw away, in one word, all the goods and gifts of fortune — that he might defend and sustain the cause which seemed to him the just one. "The victorious cause pleased the gods," and now perhaps, as victorious causes will do, it pleases the majority of men, and yet no one can withhold his admiration from the man who, though numbered among the vanquished, held his faith pure and unblemished even at the price of poverty and exile.

Upon arrival in New York on July 16, 1868, Maury was relieved to learn that President Johnson had issued a proclamation two weeks earlier grant-

ing pardon to the remaining Confederates "for the offense of treason against the United States."

After visiting relatives and friends in the New York area, Maury left for Richmond. It was a heart-breaking arrival. Although much rebuilding had been done, still the remaining ruins of this once proud Southern capital stood in mute testimony to the terrible price of war. Throughout Virginia the scene was repeated: burned-out dwellings, wasted plantations, and twisted rails.

Yes, his state still had need of Matthew Maury to

156

help her back on her feet . . . to generate his typical enthusiasm . . . to help dispel the prevailing gloom that gripped so many people.

Nor did the state forget the honor due her illustrious son. A much-appreciated part of his welcome consisted of invitations from several of Virginia's hot-springs resorts (now in West Virginia) to come and bring his family as guests of the establishment. His favorite was White Sulphur Springs, known as "The White," which he had often visited during his Washington days to escape summer malaria attacks.

Now he was delighted to find many of his old friends and ex-Confederate leaders gathered there during the summer of 1868. He could renew his old friendship with Robert E. Lee, whom he had known and respected since they were both on duty together in Washington. Lee was to become president of Washington College (later Washington and Lee University), next door to Maury's own Virginia Military Institute in Lexington. The two would be spending many pleasant hours together.

Best of all, he was able to arouse interest in and begin work on his Physical Survey of the State of Virginia. The men who worked with him on this project would later be carrying out his ideas of attracting industry to the state, of utilizing the state's water power for mills, of developing the Hampton Roads area into one of the country's great harbors, and of linking the state with the West by rail.

In September Maury and his family left for Lexington, a picturesque college town on the west side of the Blue Ridge Mountains. The train carried them as far as Goshen, where they boarded a stage for the remainder of the journey. As the vehicle rumbled along mountain roads, Maury let himself relax and enjoy the scenery as he had not done in many years. Soon they were in Goshen Pass high above the spectacular gorge of the North River. The smell of autumn was in the air, and scarlet leaves contrasted gaily with the glistening green of the mountain laurel and rhododendron. The spell of the lovely glen filled Maury with a peace he had not known for seven years. His beloved state — there was no place on earth like it.

Once installed in his new position, Maury found himself busier than ever. Lecturing to the cadets of V.M.I. was only one of his duties. Most important was the Physical Survey, which he started by issuing questionnaires to farmers and businessmen around the state. Then he set out on a series of lecturing tours to encourage the improvements he had outlined. He wanted farmers to band together to build better roads for transporting their produce to market more easily. He attempted to interest them in scientific agriculture to help make up for the loss of their Negro laborers. Encouraging European farmers to emigrate to Virginia was another of his schemes. The results of his speeches and his preliminary reports stirred much interest among Northern investors. Yet they were slow to act, because of the bitterness still prevailing between North and South.

Meanwhile, Maury at sixty-four was beginning to feel the adverse effects of the cold mountain winters at Lexington. Rheumatism affected his hands and his bad knee, forcing him to use crutches again. He was tempted by several offers of college presidencies, especially one from the University of Alabama because of its milder climate. But each time he refused, believing his own state had greater need of his services.

Then in 1871, V.M.I. ran out of money to complete the Physical Survey or even to publish Maury's next report. With time on his hands and a mind as active as ever, Maury decided to begin again where he had left off before the war, on his campaign for a central weather bureau and crop reports for farmers. He concentrated his efforts in speeches made at county agricultural fairs, urging his listeners to write to their state governments, which in turn should press Congress to act.

Maury's influence in Washington at this time was nonexistent. In fact, Henry and Bache were more completely in control of American science than before the war. They had even succeeded in discontinuing the publication of Maury's *Sailing Directions*.

Still, Maury's ideas appealed to the common man around the country, and he continued to receive invitations to present his views before organizations like the National Agricultural Association in St. Louis. One of his most satisfying assignments was an invitation from Boston to speak before the Farmers' Club of Norfolk, Massachusetts. He was well received in this state that had earlier condemned him publicly as a traitor.

One of his daughters generally accompanied him on his speaking tours. In the fall of 1872 it was Glum (now called "Elie") who went with him to St. Louis. He was ill for most of the trip out, but would not give it up despite Elie's pleadings. Next he was scheduled to speak at Norfolk, Virginia, but Maury got only as far as Fredericksburg before collapsing. When he was finally able, the pale and deathly ill scientist returned to Lexington. Stricken with a bleeding stomach ulcer, Maury informed Nan he had come home to die.

Throughout the bleak winter of 1872–73 Maury remained confined to bed with his family around him. Even Dick had returned to the States. Maury accepted his approaching death as calmly as he had life, and thanked God for being in possession of his senses to the very end.

On February 1, 1873, Maury sent his wife and daughters out of his room. The premonition of death was strong upon him and he would not have them witness a struggle. There was none. He died peacefully fifteen minutes later with Dick holding one hand and Brave the other.

The town of Lexington went into deep mourning, with all places of business closed. The cadets held a full military funeral for their beloved professor. But Nan preferred that her husband's final resting place be Richmond. The following autumn a military procession accompanied the casket through Goshen Pass along the road Maury loved so well. There they stopped while Maury's children covered the casket with laurel leaves. On September 27, 1873, Matthew Fontaine Maury was buried in Richmond's Hollywood Cemetery near the grave of President James Monroe, who had granted him his midshipman's warrant so many years before.

In the years to follow, Maury's enemies in Washington did their best to discredit his name as a scientist. Yet the "physical geography of the sea," the branch of science he had founded, was coming into its own. The British *Challenger* Expedition from 1872 to 1876 placed an indisputable scientific foundation under the studies began by Maury, and the new science came to be called "oceanography."

Today Maury's name is honored in the Maury Highway from Lexington to Goshen, the Maury River (as the old North River at Goshen was renamed), the Maury Volcano off the coast of Brazil, and Maury Hall at the United States Naval Academy at Annapolis. A monument to Maury, Pathfinder of the Sea, stands on Richmond's Monument Avenue, a plaque marks the Richmond house where he developed the electric torpedo, a stone memorial graces Goshen Pass, and a bust of Maury stands in the Hall of Fame for Great Americans at New York University. But perhaps the best remembrance of all is the wording which appears on every modern Pilot Chart issued monthly by the United States Naval Oceanographic office:

> Founded upon the researches made in the early part of the nineteenth century by Matthew Fontaine Maury while serving as a lieutenant in the U.S. Navy.

BIBLIOGRAPHY

Bell, Frederick J. *Room to Swing a Cat.* New York, Longman's, Green & Co., 1938.

Civil War Naval Chronology, 1861-1865. 2 vols. Washington, D.C., U.S. Government Printing Office, 1962.

Corbin, Diana Fontaine Maury. *A Life of Matthew Fontaine Maury, U.S.N. and C.S.N.* London, Sampson, Low, Marston, Searle & Rivington Ltd., 1888.

Hanna, A. J. "The Role of Matthew Fontaine Maury in the Mexican Empire." *The Virginia Magazine of History and Biography,* Vol. 55, No. 2 (April 1947), pp. 105-25.

Maury, Matthew Fontaine. "On the Navigation of Cape Horn." *American Journal of Science and Arts,* Vol. XXVI (July 1834), pp. 54-63.

————. *The Physical Geography of the Sea and its Meteorology.* Cambridge, Mass., The Belknap Press of Harvard University Press, 1963.

Nordhoff, Charles. *In Yankee Windjammers.* New York, Dodd, Mead & Co., 1940.

Williams, Frances Leigh. *Matthew Fontaine Maury, Scientist of the Sea.* New Brunswick, N. J., Rutgers University Press, 1963.